ISBN 978-1-7372041-0-7   hardcover special edition

ISBN 978-1-7372041-1-4   paperback

ISBN 978-1-7372041-2-1   e-book

ISBN 978-1-7372041-3-8   audiobook

Front cover and chapter art by @BitcoinUltras.

Charts by Sanjay Mavinkurve.

Cover and interior design by Anton Khodakovsky.

www.bullishcaseforbitcoin.com

PRINTED IN THE UNITED STATES OF AMERICA

The Bullish Case for Bitcoin

VIJAY BOYAPATI

TABLE OF CONTENTS

*To Addie, Will, and Vivi, for whom I fervently believe
Bitcoin will bring about a better world*

FOREWORD

THE PANDEMIC OF 2020 UPENDED THE ECONOMY OF THE world, forcing 10 years of digital transformation into the span of months. Pure digital offerings exploded in popularity and many conventional brick-and-mortar services came to a halt. Millions of businesses and billions of people found themselves caught amid the greatest disruption of their lives.

During the second quarter of 2020, our business scrambled to adapt to the new constraints of a post-COVID world. The result was a streamlined enterprise software company with half a billion in cash and more on the way. Our immediate business challenge was resolved, but a larger threat to our survival loomed in the distance.

The United States government's policy response to the pandemic was to triple the rate of monetary inflation. In essence, the cost of capital exceeded 20 percent, while the returns we could expect from any conventional treasury investment strategy were 0 percent. This made our cash stockpile and future cash flows a weight around our neck. A stable, profitable value stock growing substantially slower than the rate of monetary inflation does not serve as a store of value and rapidly loses the support of the investment community.

This problem had existed for a decade leading up the pandemic, albeit at a lower level of intensity. From 2010 through 2019, the rate of monetary inflation was approximately 7 percent and investors relentlessly pressured CEOs and CFOs to grow their cash flows in excess of this rate by any means necessary. That often meant taking on debt and using all free cash flows to buy back stock or to enter into serial acquisitions with a combination of debt and equity in order to keep revenues and expected income growing faster than this hurdle rate. The acquisitions were generally dilutive over the long term, and as management teams struggled to integrate acquisition targets, they lost focus on their core business. When each business became fully leveraged on debt, or when there were no more acquisitions to be had, it reached the end of the line.

The 7 percent hurdle rate resulted in a 99 percent mortality rate during the 20 years after our firm became public, driving one corporation after another to reach beyond their fingertips, impairing their balance sheet with too much debt and convoluting their profit and loss statements with too many disparate business units. When the hurdle rate tripled in the second quarter of 2020, it became clear that we could no longer "soldier on" with this inflationary burden hanging over our head. If we continued with business as usual, then the value created by millions of activities from thousands of employees each year would be significantly undermined by the decision of a few central bankers to print more money. The road to serfdom consists of working exponentially harder for a currency growing exponentially weaker.

The solution to our problem presented itself in the form of a K-shaped recovery. In essence, Wall Street recovered quickly due to monetary stimulus, while Main Street continued to deteriorate. The key to economic vitality in times of great monetary inflation is a large balance sheet of assets that appreciate faster than the rate of currency debasement. Accordingly, we set off on a search for the right asset mix to place on our balance sheet in lieu of cash and treasury bonds. It was during this search that we discovered Bitcoin and this wonderful thesis crafted by Vijay Boyapati.

The Bullish Case for Bitcoin, first published as a long-form article, represents an intellectual tour de force delivered with elegance and prescience by a polymath well-versed in mathematics, computer science, economics, philosophy, politics, and engineering. After March of 2020, it was evident to me that the world needed a new money based on technology. However, in February 2018, when Boyapati first published his paper, this insight required much greater perspicacity, courage, and conviction.

In a clear and concise manner, Boyapati presents the theory of money, the anatomy of Bitcoin, the reasons it is superior to the gold and fiat standards that came before it, and the promise that it offers to human civilization. He describes path dependence and the trajectory of a newly monetizing asset in terms the layman can understand, and he addresses the concerns that most commonly arise as newcomers struggle to comprehend the essence and significance of this first digital monetary network. I was immediately captivated by "The Bullish Case for Bitcoin" when I first read it and made it part of the recommended reading for all the officers and directors of my firm as we educated ourselves on Bitcoin and considered the logical path forward. In this book Boyapati updates and significantly expands on the ideas presented in his original article.

In the third quarter of 2020, MicroStrategy decided to adopt Bitcoin as our primary treasury reserve asset, becoming the first publicly traded company to convert to a Bitcoin Standard, and we eventually acquired billions of dollars' worth of Bitcoin. We recommend *The Bullish Case for Bitcoin* to any of our employees, shareholders, or constituents wishing to understand the premise and promise of Bitcoin, both as a digital treasury asset and as the world's first digital monetary network. I hope you benefit from this work as much as we did.

MICHAEL J. SAYLOR
Chairman and CEO
MicroStrategy
Miami Beach, Florida
March 27, 2021

PROLOGUE

PROMETHEUS

THE MYSTERIOUS ORIGINS OF BITCOIN SEEM TOO IMPROBABLE to be real. While the full details may never be known, we know they went something like this: on January 3, 2009, an unidentified person in an unknown location tapped a key on a computer keyboard and initiated one of the most important programs in history. The computer began searching for a particular pattern known as a hash, a digital needle in a haystack, that would secure the first block in a ledger of financial transactions now known as the blockchain. Within a few minutes or hours—no one knows for sure how long—the first hash was found, thereby completing the genesis block and bringing to life the world's first truly decentralized digital currency. Remarkably, the identity of the enigmatic figure who created Bitcoin remains unknown, even to this day. All we know is their pseudonym: Satoshi Nakamoto.

Barely two months earlier, on October 31, 2008, Nakamoto had announced a technical specification for Bitcoin to the cryptography mailing list, an email list for people interested in the study of codes and code-breaking.[1]

---

1   http://bullishcaseforbitcoin.com/references/bitcoin-announcement

Many of the members of the list referred to themselves as cypherpunks and were determined to reshape society and liberate it from the state using the privacy-enhancing tools of cryptography. Nakamoto's email was his very first post to the list, and it received little fanfare and general skepticism after it was posted. Even among this group, steeped in the history of attempts to invent a digital currency, few understood the significance of Nakamoto's email announcement. One exception was Hal Finney, a gifted cryptographer and computer scientist who had devoted much of his career to the creation of a digital currency and who was familiar with the inherent difficulties of doing so. Of the announcement of Bitcoin, Finney later recounted:

> When Satoshi announced Bitcoin on the cryptography mailing list, he got a skeptical reception at best. Cryptographers have seen too many grand schemes by clueless noobs. They tend to have a knee jerk reaction.[2]

Finney tragically passed away on August 28, 2014 from complications of Lou Gehrig's disease. He had made numerous important contributions to the development of a digital currency, especially to Bitcoin.

---

2   http://bullishcaseforbitcoin.com/references/finney-skepticism

THE GORDIAN KNOT

Ever since Tim May, a retired Intel scientist and founder of the cypherpunk movement, had presented *The Crypto Anarchist Manifesto* to a small gathering of like-minded radicals in Silicon Valley in 1992, cypherpunks had understood the critical importance of developing a digital, stateless form of money. As May wrote in his manifesto:

> Computer technology is on the verge of providing the ability for individuals and groups to communicate and interact with each other in a totally anonymous manner. Two persons may exchange messages, conduct business, and negotiate electronic contracts without ever knowing the True Name, or legal identity, of the other.[3]

Yet for business to be conducted, money is required. Money is the most important good in any developed economy because it acts as the foundation for all trade and savings. Gold, the ancient and venerable precious metal, had served this role for millennia, but its physicality was an Achilles' heel that made it vulnerable to centralization, confiscation, and state attack. Gold's status as global money was eventually repealed during the twentieth century as the state came to dominate the issuance and management of money. With a desire to facilitate anonymous payments and to overcome the vulnerabilities of gold, cypherpunks

---

3   http://bullishcaseforbitcoin.com/references/anarchist-manifesto

hoped to develop a digital currency that would be immune to the coercive power of the state.

In 1983, American computer scientist David Chaum published a design for eCash, which was the first attempt to create a system that protected the financial privacy of its users with cryptography. In 1989, Chaum founded a company called DigiCash to commercialize his invention, but it was never a financial success. Moreover, because eCash was tied to the company that created it, it suffered from the problem of centralization: if money is issued by a central authority, then that authority represents a single point of failure. And, indeed, the eCash system was shut down when DigiCash went bankrupt in 1998. Thus, the creation of a digital form of money that had no central authority was a key challenge occupying some of the most talented cryptographers and cypherpunks during the 1990s.

While meaningful progress on the development of digital currency was made by cypherpunks such as Adam Back, Nick Szabo, and Wei Dai during the late 90s, a crucial problem remained unsolved: how can digital scarcity be maintained when there is no central authority to enforce it? It had been recognized as early as the sixteenth century by the Spanish School of Salamanca that money's value derives from its scarcity. However, in the digital realm, where data can be cheaply copied and transmitted, scarcity had so far only been possible through the use of state power, as in the case of intellectual property.

British cryptographer Adam Back's HashCash system,

invented in 1997, contributed a key concept that was necessary to the development of a workable system of digital scarcity: proof-of-work. Originally intended to mitigate the increasingly expensive problem of email spam, Back proposed a system whereby a computer sought for a hash that could only be found by an exhaustive search, requiring energy to be expended, hence costing money. Once produced, a hash could quickly and cheaply be verified as authentic and used as a measure of how much energy had been expended and at approximately what cost. A hash was, in essence, a cryptographic proof that work had been done. Under Back's scheme, email senders would be required to attach a unique hash to each email to prove that some negligible cost, such as a hundredth of a penny, had been incurred. The cost would not affect regular usage but would make the ability to send spam emails en masse cost-prohibitive. Unfortunately, HashCash was not commercially successful and was missing essential elements that would allow it to function as money. Proof-of-work, however, would prove to be crucial in allowing for the coordination of untrusted parties in a decentralized system.

In 1998, American computer engineer Wei Dai proposed a system known as b-money that addressed the critical flaw of Chaum's eCash: its centralization. Instead of requiring a central authority to maintain a limited supply of money, Dai envisaged a distributed system where participants in the network would each separately maintain a ledger of how much money each participant currently had so that state coercion of any particular participant would be ineffective. Dai's proposal was impractical, however, in assuming that communication channels remain near-instant, connected, and untamperable. His system was never implemented.

The same year that Dai proposed b-money, American polymath Nick Szabo designed another system for digital money known as bit gold. As with b-money, bit gold was never implemented, but Szabo's system made a critical leap forward by reframing the problem of scarcity not as the dearth of a physical substance, but as the quality of being verifiably expensive to produce. His neologism for this quality was "unforgeable costliness." Szabo's bit gold built upon Adam Back's proof-of-work insight and allowed users of the system to mint tokens by providing a hash whose unforgeable costliness would act as a limiting factor to the increase in money supply. Ownership of such tokens would be tracked by a registry distributed across many computers known as a property club, somewhat resembling Dai's b-money but differing in its functional details.

Although tantalizingly close to a solution for decentralized money, Szabo's design suffered some important drawbacks. First, as computers continued to improve in processing power, a hash produced in the past would be easier to produce in the present, meaning that hashes produced at different points in time would not be equivalent in perceived value, breaking an important property of money called fungibility. Thus, bit gold would create a digital commodity more akin to diamonds—irregular in shape and quality and not easily interchangeable with each other—than to gold. Secondly, the concept of an ownership registry was vulnerable to Sybil attacks that would subvert the system by creating numerous fake property-club members who could then report false balances, crediting the attacker with money they did not have. While Szabo devised solutions to these problems, they were complex, and bit gold remained only theoretical.

As one century gave way to the next, hope dwindled in the cypherpunk dream for a decentralized digital currency. Hal Finney, who had paid close attention to each of the attempts to create a stateless form of money, attempted to resurrect the dream in 2004 when he designed a system known as RPOW (Reusable Proofs of Work) that was a simplified version of Szabo's bit gold. Unlike Szabo or Dai, Finney implemented a working prototype of his system, but RPOW suffered from a similar problem to Chaum's eCash by relying on a central authority. Finney attempted to mitigate the problem of centralization by replacing the central authority with an untamperable hardware device that could remotely attest to the correct balance information for users in the system. The hardware device would be more trustworthy than a coercible company, but it could still easily be turned off.

By 2008, as the world plunged into the worst economic crisis in generations, most members of the cryptography mailing list had concluded that creating a decentralized digital currency was probably impossible. Accordingly, when Satoshi Nakamoto confidently announced that he had solved the problems of decentralized money, very few members of the list took him seriously.

THE BREAKTHROUGH

A few weeks after the announcement of Bitcoin, Hal Finney began peppering Satoshi Nakamoto with questions about his new invention. Finney had quickly recognized the brilliance of Bitcoin and the ingenious imaginative leap Nakamoto had made to create a new form of digital money with no central point of authority. None of the component ideas of Bitcoin were new, nor was any of the cryptography novel, but Nakamoto had arranged the system in a perfect balance of economic incentives and cryptographic guarantees.

As part of his design, Nakamoto had solved a fundamental problem of computer science, first posed in the late 1970s, known as the Byzantine Generals Problem: how can disparate parties that do not trust each other and may even be antagonistic coordinate to achieve a shared goal, without relying on a mutually trusted intermediary? As Nick Szabo explained in 2011:

> Nakamoto improved a significant security shortcoming that my design [of bit gold] had, namely by requiring a proof-of-work to be a node in the Byzantine-resilient peer-to-peer system to lessen the threat of an untrustworthy party controlling

the majority of nodes and thus corrupting a number of important security features. Yet another feature obvious in hindsight, quite non-obvious in foresight.[4]

It was a major technical breakthrough, and although it was not immediately obvious to most members of the cryptography mailing list on October 31, 2008, Satoshi Nakamoto's invention would eventually change the world.

---

4   http://bullishcaseforbitcoin.com/references/szabo-bit-gold

CHAPTER 1

GENESIS AND THE ORIGINS OF MONEY

WITH THE MARKET CAPITALIZATION OF BITCOIN SURPASSING a trillion dollars, the bullish case for investors might seem so obvious that it does not need stating. Alternatively, it may seem foolish to invest in a digital asset that is not backed by any commodity or government and whose price rise has prompted some to compare it to the tulip mania or the dot-com bubble. Neither is true; the bullish case for Bitcoin is compelling but far from obvious. There are significant risks to investing in Bitcoin, but, as I will argue, there is still an immense opportunity.

GENESIS

Never in the history of the world had it been possible to transfer value between distant parties without relying on a trusted intermediary such as a bank or government. In 2008, Satoshi Nakamoto, whose identity remains unknown, published a nine-page solution to a long-standing problem of computer science known as the Byzantine Generals Problem.[5] Nakamoto's solution and the system

---

5   http://bullishcaseforbitcoin.com/references/white-paper

he built from it—Bitcoin—allowed, for the first time ever, value to be transferred quickly and at great distance in a trust-minimized way. The ramifications of the creation of Bitcoin are so profound for both economics and computer science that Nakamoto should rightly qualify for both a Nobel Memorial Prize in Economics *and* the Turing Award, a dual distinction only one other person, Herbert Simon, has received.

For an investor, the salient fact of the invention of Bitcoin is the creation of a new scarce digital good—bitcoins. Bitcoins are transferable digital tokens created on the Bitcoin network in a process known as mining. Bitcoin mining is roughly analogous to gold mining, except that production follows a fixed, predictable schedule. By design, only 21 million bitcoins will ever be mined, and most of these already have been; approximately 18.7 million bitcoins have been mined at the time of writing. Every four years, the number of bitcoins produced by mining is halved, with the production of new bitcoins scheduled to end completely by the year 2140.

Bitcoins are not backed by any physical commodity, nor are they guaranteed by any government or company, which raises the obvious question for a new Bitcoin investor: why do they have any value at all? Unlike stocks, bonds, real estate, or even commodities such as oil and wheat, bitcoins cannot be valued using standard discounted-cash-flow analysis or by demand for their use in the production of higher-order goods. Bitcoins fall into an entirely different

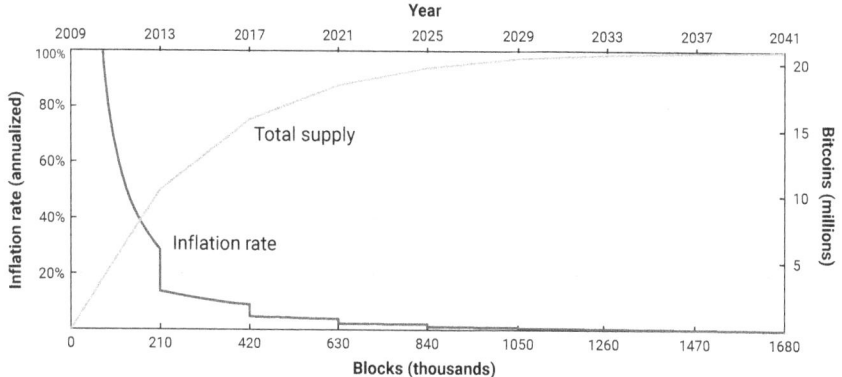

Bitcoin's inflation schedule

category of goods, known as monetary goods, whose value is set game-theoretically. That is, each market participant values the good based on their appraisal of whether and how much other participants will value it. To understand the game-theoretic nature of monetary goods, we need to explore the origins of money.

THE ORIGINS OF MONEY

In the earliest human societies, trade between groups of people occurred through barter. The incredible inefficiencies inherent to barter trade drastically limited the scale and geographical scope at which trade could occur. A major disadvantage with barter-based trade is the double coincidence of wants problem. An apple grower may desire trade with a fisherman, for example, but if the fisherman does not desire apples at the same moment, the trade will not take place. Over time, humans evolved a desire to hold certain collectible items for their rarity and symbolic value (examples include shells, animal teeth, and flint). Indeed, as Nick Szabo argues in his brilliant essay on the origins of money, the human desire for collectibles provided a distinct evolutionary advantage for early man over his nearest biological competitors, Neanderthals. Szabo writes, "[t]he primary and ultimate evolutionary function of collectibles was as a medium for storing and transferring wealth."[6]

Collectibles served as a sort of proto-money by making trade possible between otherwise antagonistic tribes and by allowing wealth to be transferred between generations. Trade and transfer of collectibles were quite infrequent in paleolithic societies, and these goods served more as a store of value rather than the medium-of-exchange role that we largely recognize modern money to play. Szabo explains:

> Compared to modern money, primitive money had a very low velocity—it might be transferred only a handful of times in an average individual's lifetime. Nevertheless, a durable collectible, what today we would call an heirloom, could persist for many generations and added substantial value at each transfer—often making the transfer even possible at all.

Early man faced an important game-theoretic dilemma when deciding which collectibles to gather or create: which objects would be desired by other humans? By correctly anticipating which objects would have collectible value, a

6   http://bullishcaseforbitcoin.com/references/shelling-out

tremendous benefit was conferred on the possessor in their ability to conduct trade and acquire wealth. Some Native American tribes, such as the Narragansetts, specialized in the manufacture of otherwise useless collectibles simply for their trade value. It is worth noting that the earlier the anticipation of future demand for a collectible good, the greater the advantage conferred to its possessor; it can be acquired more cheaply than when it is widely demanded, and its trade value appreciates as the population demanding it expands. Furthermore, acquiring a good in hopes that it will be demanded as a future store of value hastens its adoption for that very purpose. This seeming circularity is actually a feedback loop that drives societies to quickly converge on a single store of value. In game-theoretic terms, this is known as a Nash Equilibrium.[7] Achieving a Nash Equilibrium for a store of value is a major boon to any society, as it greatly facilitates trade and the division of labor, paving the way for the advancement of civilization.

Over the millennia, as human societies grew and trade routes developed, the stores of value that emerged in individual societies came to compete against each other. Merchants and traders would face a choice of whether to save the proceeds of their trade in the store of value of their own society, the store of value of the society they were trading with, or some balance of both. The benefit of maintaining savings in a foreign store of value was the enhanced ability to conduct trade in the associated foreign society.

7   http://bullishcaseforbitcoin.com/references/nash-equilibrium

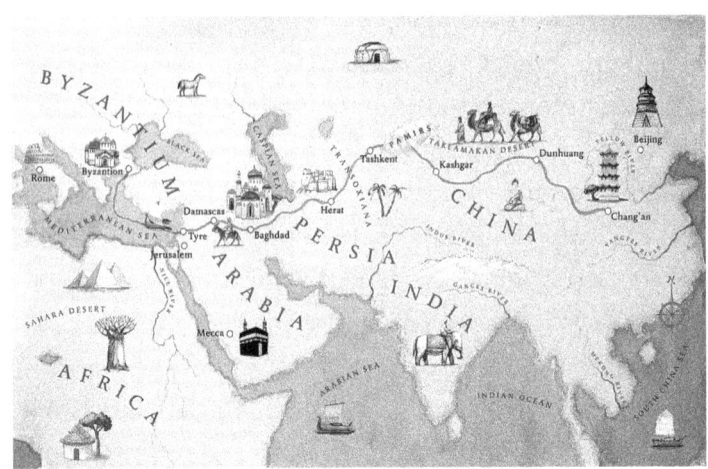

The Silk Road

Merchants holding savings in a foreign store of value also had an incentive to encourage its adoption within their own society, as this would increase the purchasing power of their savings. The benefits of an imported store of value accrued not only to the merchants doing the importing, but also to the societies themselves. Two societies converging on a single store of value would see a substantial decrease in the cost of trading with each other and an attendant increase in trade-based wealth. Indeed, the nineteenth century was the first time when most of the world converged on a single store of value, gold, and this period saw the greatest explosion of trade in the history of the world. Of this halcyon period, Lord Keynes wrote:

> What an extraordinary episode in the economic progress of man that age was ... for any man of capacity or character at all exceeding the average,

into the middle and upper classes, for whom life offered, at a low cost and with the least trouble, conveniences, comforts, and amenities beyond the compass of the richest and most powerful monarchs of other ages. The inhabitant of London could order by telephone, sipping his morning tea in bed, the various products of the whole earth, in such quantity as he might see fit, and reasonably expect their early delivery upon his doorstep.[8]

---

8   http://bullishcaseforbitcoin.com/references/lord-keynes-quote

CHAPTER 2

THE ATTRIBUTES OF A GOOD STORE OF VALUE

WHEN STORES OF VALUE COMPETE AGAINST EACH OTHER, specific attributes determine which are likely to out-compete others at the margin and win increased demand over time. Historically, many goods have been used as stores of value, and time has shown that an ideal store of value will excel in the following ways:

- **Durable**: the good must not be perishable or easily destroyed. Thus, wheat is not an ideal store of value.

- **Portable**: the good must be easy to transport and store, making it possible to secure it against loss or theft and allowing it to facilitate long-distance trade. A cow is thus less ideal than a gold bracelet.

- **Fungible**: one specimen of the good should be interchangeable with another of equal quantity. Without fungibility, the coincidence of wants problem remains unsolved. Thus, gold is better than diamonds, which are irregular in shape and quality.

- **Verifiable**: the good must be easy to quickly identify and verify as authentic. Easy verification increases the confidence of its recipient in a trade, making it more likely the trade will be consummated.

- **Divisible**: the good must be easy to subdivide. While this attribute was less important in early societies where trade was infrequent, it became more important as trade flourished and the quantities exchanged became smaller and more precise.

- **Scarce**: As Nick Szabo termed it, a monetary good must have *unforgeable costliness*. In other words, the good must not be abundant or easy to either obtain or produce in quantity. Scarcity is perhaps the most important attribute of a store of value as it taps into the innate human desire to collect that which is rare. It is the source of the original value of the store of value.

- **Established history**: the longer the good is perceived by society to have been valuable, the greater its appeal as a store of value. A long-established store of value will be hard to displace by a new upstart, except by force of conquest or if the arriviste is endowed with a significant advantage among the other attributes listed above.

- **Censorship resistant**: a new attribute, which has become increasingly important in our modern, digital society with pervasive surveillance, is censorship resistance. That is, how difficult it is for an external party such as a corporation or state to prevent the owner of the good from keeping and using it. Goods that are censorship resistant are ideal for those living under regimes that are trying to enforce capital controls or to outlaw various forms of peaceful trade.

The table below grades Bitcoin, gold, and fiat money (such as dollars) against the attributes listed above and is followed by an explanation of each grade:

	Bitcoin	Gold	Fiat
Durable	B	A+	
Portable	A+	D	B
Fungible	B	A	B
Verifiable	A+	B	B
Divisible	A+		B
Scarce	A+	A	F
Established history	D	A+	
Censorship resistant	A		D

DURABILITY

Gold is the undisputed king of durability. Most of the gold that has ever been mined or minted, including the gold of the Pharaohs, remains extant today and will likely be available a thousand years hence. Gold coins that were used as money in antiquity still maintain significant value today. Fiat currency and bitcoins are fundamentally digital records that may take physical form (such as paper bills). Thus, it is not their physical manifestation whose durability should be considered (since a tattered dollar bill may be exchanged for a new one), but rather the durability of the institution that issues them. In the case of fiat currencies, many governments have come and gone over the centuries, and their currencies disappeared with them. The Papiermark, Rentenmark, and Reichsmark of the Weimar Republic no longer have value because the institution that issued them no longer exists. If history is a guide, it would be folly to consider fiat currencies durable in the long term—the U.S. dollar and British pound are relative anomalies in this regard. Bitcoins, having no issuing authority, may be considered durable so long as the network that secures them remains in place. Given that Bitcoin is still in its infancy, it is too early to draw strong conclusions about its durability. However, there are encouraging signs that, despite prominent instances of nation-states attempting to regulate Bitcoin and years of attacks by hackers, the network has continued to function, displaying a remarkable degree of *anti-fragility*.[9]

9   http://bullishcaseforbitcoin.com/references/anti-fragility

PORTABILITY

Bitcoins are the most portable store of value ever used by man. Private keys representing hundreds of millions of dollars can be stored on a tiny USB drive and easily carried anywhere. Furthermore, equally valuable sums can be transmitted between people at opposite ends of the earth almost instantly. Fiat currencies, being fundamentally digital, are also highly portable. However, government regulations and capital controls mean that large transfers of value usually take days or may not be possible at all. Cash can be used to avoid capital controls, but then the risk of storage and cost of transportation become significant. Gold, being physical in form and incredibly dense, is by far the least portable. It is no wonder that most bullion is never transported. When bullion is traded between a buyer and a seller, it is typically only the title to the gold that is transferred, not the physical bullion itself, providing a weaker assurance of ownership for the buyer. Transporting physical gold across large distances is costly, risky, and time-consuming.

FUNGIBILITY

Gold provides the standard for fungibility. When melted down, an ounce of gold is essentially indistinguishable from any other ounce and gold has always traded this way on the market. Fiat currencies, on the other hand, are only as fungible as the issuing institutions allow them to be. While it may be the case that a fiat banknote is usually treated like any other by merchants accepting them, there are instances where large-denomination notes have been treated differently than small ones. For instance, India's government completely demonetized their 500- and 1000-rupee banknotes in an attempt to stamp out India's untaxed gray market. The demonetization caused 500- and 1000-rupee notes to trade at a discount to their face value, making them no longer truly fungible with their lower denomination sibling notes. Bitcoins are fungible at the network level, meaning that every bitcoin when transmitted is treated the same on the Bitcoin network. However, because bitcoins are traceable on the blockchain—a public record of all transactions that have ever taken place on the Bitcoin network—a particular bitcoin may become tainted by its use in illicit trade and businesses may be compelled not to accept such tainted bitcoins. Without improvements to the privacy and anonymity of Bitcoin's network protocol, bitcoins cannot be considered as fungible as gold.

VERIFIABILITY

For most intents and purposes, both fiat currencies and gold are fairly easy to verify for authenticity. However, despite providing features on their banknotes to prevent counterfeiting, nation-states and their citizens can still potentially be duped by counterfeit bills. Gold is also not immune from counterfeiting. Sophisticated criminals have used gold-plated tungsten as a way of fooling investors into paying for false gold.[10] Bitcoins, on the other hand, can be

---

10   http://bullishcaseforbitcoin.com/references/fake-gold

verified with mathematical certainty. Using cryptographic signatures, the owner of bitcoins can publicly prove they own the bitcoins they say they do.

DIVISIBILITY

Bitcoins can be divided down to a hundred millionth of a bitcoin and transmitted at such infinitesimal amounts (network fees can, however, make transmission of tiny amounts uneconomical). Fiat currencies are typically divisible down to pocket change, which has little purchasing power, making fiat divisible enough in practice. Gold, while physically divisible, becomes difficult to use when divided into small enough quantities to be suitable for lower-value, day-to-day commerce.

SCARCITY

The attribute that most clearly distinguishes Bitcoin from fiat currencies and gold is its predetermined scarcity. By design, at most 21 million bitcoins can ever be created. This gives the owner of bitcoins a known percentage of the total possible supply. For instance, an owner of 10 bitcoins would know that at most 2.1 million people on earth (less than 0.03 percent of the world's population) could ever have as many bitcoins as they had. Gold, while remaining quite scarce throughout history, is not immune to increases in supply. If it were ever the case that a new method of mining or acquiring gold became economical, the supply of gold could rise dramatically (examples include sea-floor mining[11] or asteroid mining[12]). Finally, fiat currencies, while only a relatively recent historical invention, have proven to be prone to constant increases in supply. Nation-states have shown a persistent proclivity to inflate their money supply to solve short-term political problems. The inflationary tendencies of governments across the world leave the owner of a fiat currency with the likelihood that their savings will diminish in value over time.

ESTABLISHED HISTORY

No monetary good has a history as long and storied as gold, which has been valued for as long as human civilization has existed. Coins minted in the distant days of antiquity still maintain significant value today.[13] The same cannot be said of fiat currencies, which are a relatively recent anomaly of history. From their inception, fiat currencies have had a near-universal tendency toward eventual worthlessness. The use of inflation as an insidious means of invisibly taxing a citizenry has been a temptation that few states in history have been able to resist. If the twentieth century, in which fiat monies came to dominate the global monetary order, established any economic truth, it is that fiat money cannot be trusted to maintain its value over the long or even medium term. Bitcoin, despite its short existence, has weathered enough trials in the market that there is a high likelihood it will not vanish as a valued asset any time soon.

11   http://bullishcaseforbitcoin.com/references/deep-sea-mining
12   http://bullishcaseforbitcoin.com/references/asteroid-mining
13   http://bullishcaseforbitcoin.com/references/hoxne-hoard

Furthermore, the Lindy effect suggests that the longer Bitcoin remains in existence, the greater society's confidence that it will continue to exist long into the future.[14] In other words, social trust in a new monetary good is asymptotic in nature, as is illustrated in the graph below:

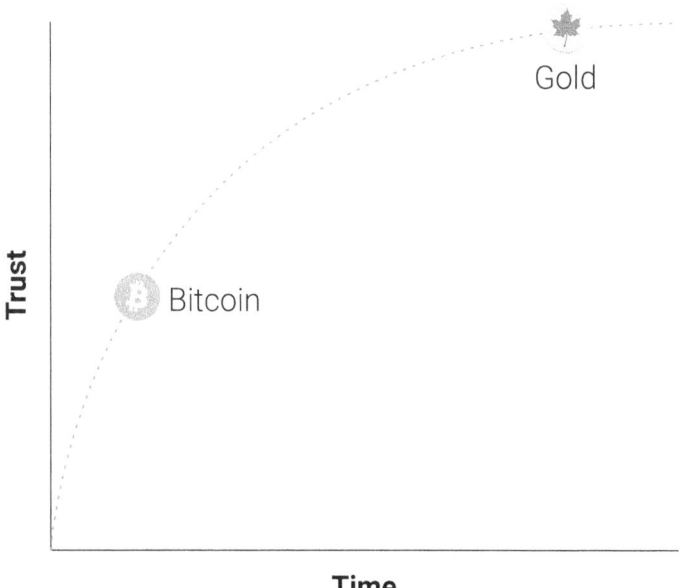

If Bitcoin exists for 20 years, there will be near-universal confidence that it will be available forever, much as people believe the Internet is a permanent feature of the modern world.

---

14   http://bullishcaseforbitcoin.com/references/lindy-effect

CENSORSHIP RESISTANCE

One of the most significant sources of early demand for bitcoins was their use in the illicit drug trade. Many subsequently surmised, mistakenly, that the primary demand for bitcoins was due to their ostensible anonymity. Bitcoin, however, is far from an anonymous currency; every transaction transmitted on the Bitcoin network is forever recorded on a public blockchain. The historical record of transactions allows for later forensic analysis to identify the source of a flow of funds. It was such an analysis that led to the apprehending of a perpetrator of the infamous MtGox heist.[15] While it is true that a sufficiently careful and diligent person can conceal their identity when using Bitcoin, this is not why Bitcoin was so popular for trading drugs. The key attribute that makes Bitcoin valuable for proscribed activities is that it is *permissionless* at the network level. When bitcoins are transmitted on the Bitcoin network, there is no human intervention deciding whether the transaction should be allowed. As a distributed peer-to-peer network, Bitcoin is, by its very nature, designed to be censorship-resistant. This is in stark contrast to the fiat banking system, where states regulate banks and the other gatekeepers of money transmission to report and prevent outlawed uses of monetary goods. A classic example of regulated money transmission is capital controls. A wealthy millionaire, for instance, may find it infeasible or risky to transfer their wealth to a new domicile if they wish to flee

15   http://bullishcaseforbitcoin.com/references/mtgox-forensics

an oppressive regime. Although gold is not issued by states, its physical nature makes it difficult to transport, making it far more susceptible to state control than Bitcoin. India's Gold Control Act is an example of such regulation.[16]

Bitcoin excels across most attributes listed above, allowing it to outcompete modern and ancient monetary goods at the margin and providing a strong incentive for its increasing adoption. In particular, the potent combination of censorship resistance and absolute scarcity has been a powerful motivator for wealthy investors to allocate a portion of their wealth to the nascent asset class.

16   http://bullishcaseforbitcoin.com/references/india-gold-act

CHAPTER 3

THE EVOLUTION OF MONEY

THERE IS AN OBSESSION IN MODERN MONETARY ECONOMICS with the medium-of-exchange role of money. In the twentieth century, states have monopolized the issuance of money and continually undermined its use as a store of value, creating a false belief that money is primarily defined as a medium of exchange. Many have criticized Bitcoin as being an unsuitable money because its price has been too volatile for it to be used as a medium of exchange. This puts the cart before the horse, however. Money has always evolved in stages, with the store-of-value role preceding the medium-of-exchange role. One of the fathers of marginalist economics, William Stanley Jevons, explained that:

> Historically speaking ... gold seems to have served, firstly, as a commodity valuable for ornamental purposes; secondly, as stored wealth; thirdly, as a medium of exchange; and, lastly, as a measure of value.[17]

---

17   http://bullishcaseforbitcoin.com/references/jevons-quote

Using modern terminology, money always evolves in the following four stages:

1. **Collectible:** In the very first stage of its evolution, money will be demanded solely based on its peculiar properties, usually becoming a whimsy of its possessor. Shells, beads, and gold were all collectibles before later transitioning to the more familiar roles of money.

2. **Store of value:** Once it is demanded by enough people for its peculiarities, money will be recognized as a means of keeping and storing value over time. As a good becomes more widely recognized as a suitable store of value, its purchasing power will rise as more people demand it for this purpose. The purchasing power of a store of value will eventually plateau when it is widely held and the influx of new people desiring it as a store of value dwindles.

3. **Medium of exchange:** When money is fully established as a store of value, its purchasing power will stabilize. Having stabilized in purchasing power, the opportunity cost of using money to conduct trade will diminish to a level suitable for use as a medium of exchange. In the earliest days of Bitcoin, many people did not appreciate the huge opportunity cost of using bitcoins as a medium of exchange, rather than

as an incipient store of value. The famous story of a man trading 10,000 bitcoins (worth approximately $480 million at the time of this book's writing) for two pizzas illustrates this confusion.[18]

4. **Unit of account:** When money is widely used as a medium of exchange, goods will be priced in terms of it. That is, the exchange ratio against money will be available for most goods. It is a common misconception that bitcoin prices are available for many goods today. For example, while a cup of coffee might be available for purchase using bitcoins, the price listed is not a true bitcoin price; rather, it is the dollar price desired by the merchant translated into bitcoin terms at the current USD/BTC market exchange rate. If the price of Bitcoin were to drop in dollar terms, the number of bitcoins requested by the merchant would increase commensurately. Only when merchants are willing to accept bitcoins for payment without regard to the bitcoin exchange rate against fiat currencies can we truly think of Bitcoin as having become a unit of account.

Monetary goods that are not yet a unit of account may be thought of as being partly monetized. Today gold fills such a role, being a store of value but having been stripped of its medium-of-exchange and unit-of-account roles by

---

18   http://bullishcaseforbitcoin.com/references/pizza-story

government intervention. It is also possible that one good fills the medium-of-exchange role of money while another good fills the other roles. This is typically true in countries with dysfunctional states, such as Argentina or Zimbabwe. In his book *Digital Gold*, Nathaniel Popper writes:

> In America, the dollar seamlessly serves the three functions of money: providing a medium of exchange, a unit for measuring the cost of goods, and an asset where value can be stored. In Argentina, on the other hand, while the peso was used as a medium of exchange—for daily purchases—no one used it as a store of value. Keeping savings in the peso was equivalent to throwing away money. So people exchanged any pesos they wanted to save for dollars, which kept their value better than the peso. Because the peso was so volatile, people usually remembered prices in dollars, which provided a more reliable unit of measure over time.

Bitcoin is currently transitioning from the first stage of monetization (collectible) to the second stage (store of value). It will likely be several years before Bitcoin transitions from being an incipient store of value to being a true medium of exchange, and the path it takes to get there is still fraught with risk and uncertainty. It is striking to note that the same transition took many centuries for gold. No one alive has seen the real-time monetization of a good (as is taking place with Bitcoin), so there is precious little experience regarding the path this monetization will take.

PATH DEPENDENCE

In the process of being monetized, a monetary good will soar in purchasing power. Many have commented that the increase in purchasing power of Bitcoin creates the appearance of a bubble. While this term is often used disparagingly to suggest that Bitcoin is grossly overvalued, it is unintentionally apt. A characteristic that is common to all monetary goods is that their purchasing power is higher than can be justified by their use-value alone. Indeed, many historical monies had no use-value at all. The difference between the purchasing power of a monetary good and the exchange-value it could command for its inherent usefulness can be thought of as a monetary premium. As a monetary good transitions through the stages of monetization (listed in the prior section), the monetary premium will increase. The premium does not, however, move in a straight, predictable line. A good X that was in the process of being monetized may be outcompeted by another good Y that is more suitable as money, and the monetary premium of X may drop or vanish entirely. The monetary premium of silver disappeared almost entirely in the late nineteenth century when governments across the world largely abandoned it as money in favor of gold.

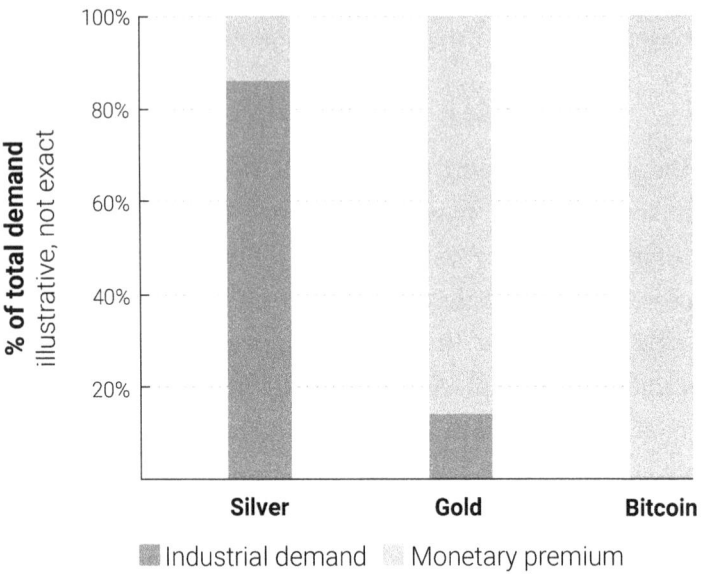

Monetary premium of different monetary goods

■ Industrial demand   Monetary premium

Even in the absence of exogenous factors such as government intervention or competition from other monetary goods, the monetary premium for a new money will not follow a predictable path. Economist Larry White observed that "the trouble with [the] bubble story, of course, is that [it] is consistent with any price path, and thus gives no explanation for a particular price path."[19]

The process of monetization is game-theoretic; every market participant attempts to anticipate the aggregate demand of other participants and thereby the future monetary premium. Because the monetary premium is unanchored to any inherent usefulness, market participants

19   http://bullishcaseforbitcoin.com/references/path-dependence

tend to default to past prices when determining whether a monetary good is cheap or expensive and whether to buy or sell it. The connection of current demand to past prices is known as path dependence and is perhaps the greatest source of confusion in understanding the price movements of monetary goods.

When the purchasing power of a monetary good increases with increasing adoption, market expectations of what constitutes "cheap" and "expensive" shift accordingly. Similarly, when the price of a monetary good crashes, expectations can switch to a general belief that prior prices were "irrational" or overly inflated. The path dependence of money is illustrated by the words of well-known Wall Street fund manager Josh Brown:

> I bought [bitcoins] at like $2300 and had an immediate double on my hands. Then I started saying "I can't buy more of it," as it rose, even though that's an anchored opinion based on nothing other than the price where I originally got it. Then, as it fell over the last week because of a Chinese crackdown on the exchanges, I started saying to myself, "Oh good, I hope it gets killed so I can buy more."[20]

The truth is that the notions of "cheap" and "expensive" are essentially meaningless in reference to monetary goods. The price of a monetary good is not a reflection of

20   http://bullishcaseforbitcoin.com/references/josh-brown-quote

its cash flow or how useful it is but, rather, is a measure of how widely adopted it has become for the various roles of money.

Further complicating the path-dependent nature of money is the fact that market participants do not merely act as dispassionate observers, trying to buy or sell in anticipation of future movements of the monetary premium, but also act as active evangelizers. Since there is no objectively correct monetary premium, proselytizing the superior attributes of a monetary good is more effective than for regular goods, whose value is ultimately anchored to cash flow or use-demand. The religious fervor of participants in the Bitcoin market can be observed in various online forums where owners actively promote the benefits of Bitcoin and the wealth that can be made by investing in it. In observing the Bitcoin market, Leigh Drogen comments:

> You recognize this as a religion—a story we all tell each other and agree upon. Religion is the adoption curve we ought to be thinking about. It's almost perfect—as soon as someone gets in, they tell everyone and go out evangelizing. Then their friends get in and they start evangelizing.[21]

While the comparison to religion may give Bitcoin an aura of irrational faith, it is entirely rational for the individual owner to evangelize for a superior monetary good and

---

21   http://bullishcaseforbitcoin.com/references/leigh-drogen-quote

for a society to standardize on it. Money acts as the foundation for all trade and savings, so the adoption of a superior form of money has tremendous multiplicative benefits to wealth creation for all members of a society.

CHAPTER 4

THE SHAPE OF MONETIZATION

HYPE CYCLES

WHILE THERE ARE NO *A PRIORI* RULES FOR THE PATH A MONetary good will take as it is monetized, a curious pattern has emerged during the relatively brief history of Bitcoin's monetization. Bitcoin's price appears to follow a fractal pattern of increasing magnitude, where each iteration of the fractal matches the classic shape of a Gartner hype cycle, as illustrated in the chart on the next page.

In his article "Speculative Bitcoin Adoption/Price Theory," Michael Casey posits that the expanding Gartner hype cycles represent phases of a standard S-curve of adoption that was followed by many transformative technologies as they become commonly used in society.[22]

Each Gartner hype cycle begins with a burst of enthusiasm for the new technology, and the price is bid up by the market participants who are "reachable" in that iteration. The earliest buyers in a Gartner hype cycle typically have a strong conviction about the transformative nature of the

---

22   http://bullishcaseforbitcoin.com/references/speculative-adoption-theory

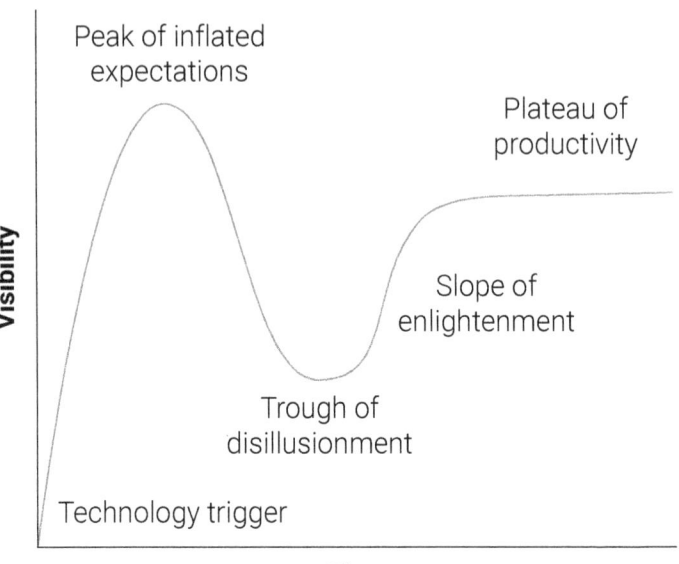

Peak of inflated expectations

Plateau of productivity

Visibility

Slope of enlightenment

Trough of disillusionment

Technology trigger

Time

technology they are investing in. Eventually, the market reaches a climax of enthusiasm as the supply of new participants who can be reached in the cycle is exhausted, and the buying becomes dominated by speculators more interested in quick profits than the underlying technology.

Following the peak of the hype cycle, prices rapidly drop, and speculative fervor is replaced by despair, public derision, and a sense that the technology was not transformative at all. Eventually the price bottoms and forms a plateau where the original investors who had strong conviction are joined by a new cohort who were able to withstand the pain of the crash and who appreciated the importance of the technology.

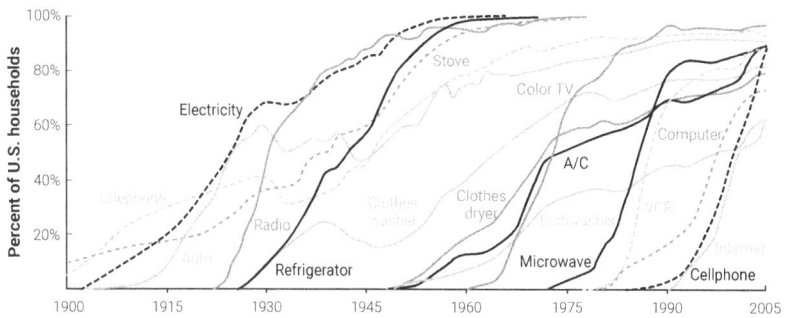

Adoption curves of various consumer goods

The plateau persists for a prolonged period and forms, as Casey calls it, a "stable, boring low." During the plateau, public interest in the technology will dwindle, but it will continue to be developed, and the collection of strong believers will slowly grow. A new base is then set for the next iteration of the hype cycle as external observers recognize the technology is not going away and that investing in it may not be as risky as it seemed during the crash phase of the cycle. The next iteration of the hype cycle will bring in a much larger set of adopters and be far greater in magnitude.

Very few people participating in an iteration of a Gartner hype cycle will correctly anticipate how high prices will go in that cycle. Prices usually reach levels that would seem absurd to most investors at the earliest stages of the cycle. When the cycle ends, a popular cause is typically attributed to the crash by the media. While the stated cause, such as an exchange failure, may be a precipitating event, it is not the fundamental reason for the cycle to end. Gartner hype cycles end because of an exhaustion of market participants reachable in the cycle.

$1600
$1200
$800
Gold price
$400

1980   1990   2000   2010

It is telling that gold followed the classic pattern of a Gartner hype cycle from the late 1970s to the early 2000s. One might speculate that the hype cycle is a social dynamic inherent to the process of monetization.

GARTNER COHORTS

Prior to the launch of the MtGox exchange in July 2010, no hype cycles were discernible in Bitcoin's minuscule market. The market was dominated by a coterie of cryptographers, computer scientists, and cypherpunks who were already primed to understand the importance of Satoshi Nakamoto's groundbreaking invention and who were pioneers in establishing that the Bitcoin protocol was free of technical flaws. Prices were set either by direct exchange or by barter transactions, such as the purchase of two pizzas for 10,000 bitcoins by Laszlo Hanyecz. Bitcoin's price in these early days remained well below $1.

After the establishment of the first exchange-traded price in 2010, Bitcoin's market has witnessed four major Gartner hype cycles. With hindsight, we can precisely identify the price ranges of previous hype cycles in the Bitcoin market. We can also qualitatively identify the cohort of investors associated with each iteration of prior cycles.

$0.06–$30 (July 2010–July 2011): The first cycle attracted a steady stream of ideologically motivated investors who were dazzled by the potential of a stateless, digital money. Libertarians such as Roger Ver and Ross Ulbricht were attracted to Bitcoin for the anti-establishment activities that would become possible if the nascent technology became widely adopted. The cycle reached its climax just a month after *Gawker* published a widely read article covering Bitcoin and its use in a website known as Silk Road that had been created by Ulbricht. Silk Road facilitated the purchase of illicit substances using bitcoins and was an early source of demand for the digital currency.

$30–$1,154 (August 2011–December 2013): The second cycle saw the entrance of the most intrepid of investors, such as the Argentinian Wences Casares, who were willing to take a chance on the iconoclastic and unproven technology. Casares saw in Bitcoin a potential cure for the economic ravages of the hyperinflation he had experienced as a child. A brilliant and well-connected serial entrepreneur, Casares is known to have evangelized Bitcoin to some of the most prominent technologists and investors in Silicon Valley, and he came to be known as patient zero for spreading the so-called "mind virus" in this way.

The Winklevoss twins, who had tussled with Mark Zuckerberg about the founding of Facebook and had received a large settlement from the company, were also participants in the second hype cycle. Having received a large payout from Facebook, the Winklevoss twins were celebrating in Ibiza when a chance encounter with investor David Azar first exposed them to this new investment opportunity. They were immediately intrigued by what they heard and eventually used their newfound capital to invest in Bitcoin.

Investors in Bitcoin's first and second hype cycles were willing to brave the arcane and risky liquidity channels from which bitcoins could be acquired. The primary source of liquidity in the market during this period was the Japan-based MtGox exchange that was run by the notoriously incompetent and malfeasant Mark Karpeles, who later received a prison sentence for his culpability in the collapse of the exchange.

$1,154–$19,600 (January 2014–December 2017): The third hype cycle attracted the first major influx of investors without an ideological affinity to the cypherpunk ethos that gave rise to Bitcoin. In terms of the S-curve of adoption, these new investors could be recognized as "early adopters" (see chart on the next page).

An analysis of blockchain and exchange data from this period by Willy Woo suggests that the cohort of new entrants was dominated by retail investors and that global usage grew from approximately 1-2 million investors to over 14 million.[23] The cycle ended with a speculative fervor

23   http://bullishcaseforbitcoin.com/references/willy-woo-data

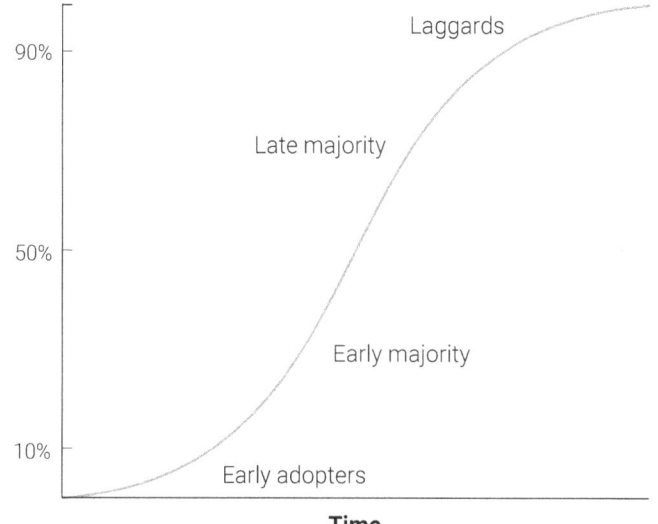

driven by the launch of a legion of alternative cryptocurrencies (alt-coins) competing with Bitcoin for market dominance. The vast majority of these alt-coins have since faded into obsolescence.

It is worth observing that the rise in Bitcoin's price during the aforementioned hype cycles was largely correlated with an increase in liquidity and the ease with which investors could purchase bitcoins. In the first two hype cycles, MtGox was the primary source of Bitcoin's liquidity and obtaining and securing bitcoins from this poorly run exchange remained too complex for all but the most technologically savvy investors. Furthermore, many who did manage to transfer money to MtGox ultimately faced loss of funds when the exchange was hacked and later closed. By the beginning of the third hype cycle, competitors to

MtGox began to emerge. However, even after MtGox's collapse and replacement by more competent competitors, significant hurdles remained for investors seeking to invest in Bitcoin. Banks were often reluctant to deal with exchanges and exchanges such as Coinbase were unable to keep their service consistently available under heavy usage. The newly emerging financial infrastructure remained rickety at best.

It was only after the end of the third hype cycle and a two-year lull in the market price of Bitcoin that mature and deep sources of liquidity were developed; examples include OTC brokers, regulated exchanges that improved their reliability and futures markets such as the Chicago Mercantile Exchange. By the time the fourth hype cycle began in 2020, it was relatively easy for retail and institutional investors to buy and secure bitcoins.

$19600—? (January 2018 – ?): At the time of writing, the Bitcoin market is undergoing its fourth major hype cycle. As sources of liquidity have deepened and matured, major institutional investors can now participate and indeed several prominent wealth managers such as Paul Tudor Jones and Stanley Druckenmiller have allocated a portion of their funds to Bitcoin. Along with wealth management funds, public companies Tesla, MicroStrategy, and Square have apportioned part, or all in the case of MicroStrategy, of their corporate treasuries to Bitcoin, setting a precedent for other large corporations to do the same.

With the maturation of Bitcoin's market, institutional

demand is likely to play a powerful role in the current hype cycle. As Philip Gradwell, CEO of blockchain analytics firm Chainalysis, wrote in a note to clients:

> The role of institutional investors is becoming ever clearer in the data ... Demand is being driven by North American investors on fiat exchanges, with greater demand from institutional buyers.[24]

A study produced by the University of Cambridge Center for Alternative Finance concluded that, by the third quarter of 2020, there were "a total of up to 101 million unique crypto asset users" globally.[25] It appears that during the current hype cycle, Bitcoin is poised to shift from the "early adopters" phase of the S-curve of global adoption to the "early majority." The availability of a regulated futures market paves the way for the eventual creation of a Bitcoin ETF, which will then usher in the "late majority" and "laggards" in subsequent hype cycles.

Although it is impossible to predict the exact magnitude of the current hype cycle, it would be reasonable to conjecture that in the current cycle Bitcoin attains some significant fraction of the market capitalization of gold—its closest cousin in the global family of financial assets.

24 http://bullishcaseforbitcoin.com/references/gradwell-quote
25 http://bullishcaseforbitcoin.com/references/benchmarking-study

THE EFFECT OF THE HALVING

Bitcoins are produced by a competitive process known as mining that requires the expenditure of computational energy. The Bitcoin production schedule is predetermined by its protocol and, by design, approximately every 10 minutes a new block is mined by a miner (a computer participating on the Bitcoin network). Each time a miner successfully mines a block it is awarded a fixed number of bitcoins, and this reward is known as the block subsidy. The block subsidy is the original source of all bitcoins produced on the Bitcoin network.

Approximately every four years or, more precisely, once every 210,000 blocks, the Bitcoin block subsidy is halved in an event known as the halving. For the first four years of Bitcoin's existence, each block carried a reward of 50 bitcoins. For the next four years, the block subsidy was 25 bitcoins. In the current epoch, which began in May 2020, each block rewards miners with just 6.25 bitcoins. By the year 2140, or thereabouts, the block subsidy will decline to zero and no new bitcoins will be produced by mining. An important question for investors is what affect Bitcoin halvings have on its price level and whether this quadrennial supply shock can be adequately "priced in" by the market.

Bitcoin's protocol specifies that the amount of computational energy required to mine a block is adjusted periodically to maintain a relatively consistent output of bitcoins during each halving epoch. If the computational resources devoted to mining increase, the difficulty of mining is adjusted upward, and it becomes more costly to mine new bitcoins. This difficulty adjustment tends to make miners into marginal producers. That is, the profit from mining tends toward zero over time. Due to the marginal nature of the mining business, miners typically need to sell most of the bitcoins they mine to cover the continuing costs of running their operations, which are dominated by electricity costs. Thus, miners provide a constant downward pressure on Bitcoin's price level. When the Bitcoin halving occurs, the downward selling pressure of miners is approximately halved in magnitude.

All things being equal, if demand for bitcoins were to remain constant, the halving would result in an excess of demand over supply, causing the price to rise. Given the predetermined timing of each halving, it seems that it should be possible for market participants to anticipate the event and price it in. Yet historically, it is clear that Bitcoin halvings have not been adequately priced in and that Bitcoin's price seems to rise dramatically after each halving. Indeed, it may be speculated that Bitcoin's halving is the *precipitating* cause of Bitcoin's periodic hype cycles.

As we saw earlier in this chapter, when a Bitcoin hype cycle ends, the price drops precipitously until it finds an equilibrium where demand from buyers with strong conviction matches the supply from speculators seeking to exit the market and miners selling to cover their cost of production. The halving disrupts the eventual equilibrium, and the supply of bitcoins that are tradeable on the market is slowly but surely transferred to the hands of long-term holders. As the pool of tradeable bitcoins diminishes, the market price of Bitcoin begins to drift upward, and the apparently inexorable rise in price seems to trigger a classic "madness of crowds" phenomenon and the parabolic phase of the hype cycle ensues.

A potential reason that prior halvings have historically not been priced in is that when a halving triggers a new hype cycle, it is unclear how large the cohort of participants reachable in that hype cycle will be, and to what extent members of the cohort will be willing to allocate their savings to Bitcoin. Complicating matters are the complex feedback loops involved in monetization. We have already noted that when some investors decide to save in Bitcoin they not only act as passive investors, but also become active evangelizers for the superiority of Bitcoin as a means of saving to others. The extent to which this evangelization enlarges a cohort is perhaps not measurable.

THE ENTRANCE OF NATION-STATES

Bitcoin's final Gartner hype cycle will begin when nation-states start accumulating it as a part of their foreign currency reserves. The market capitalization of Bitcoin is currently too small for it to be considered a viable addition to reserves for most countries. However, as private sector interest increases and the capitalization of Bitcoin approaches that of gold, it will become liquid enough for most states to enter the market. The entrance of the first state to officially add bitcoins to their reserves will likely trigger a stampede for others to do so. The states that are the earliest in adopting Bitcoin would see the largest benefit to their balance sheets if Bitcoin ultimately became a global reserve currency. Unfortunately, it will probably be states with the strongest executive powers, such as dictatorships like North Korea, that will be the earliest to accumulate bitcoins. The unwillingness to see such states improve their financial position and the inherently weak executive branches of the Western democracies will cause them to dither and lag behind in accumulating bitcoins for their reserves.

There is a great irony that the United States is currently one of the nations most open in its regulatory position toward Bitcoin, while China and Russia are the most hostile. The U.S. risks the greatest downside to its geopolitical position if Bitcoin were to supplant the dollar as the world's reserve currency. In the 1960s, Charles de Gaulle criticized the "exorbitant privilege" the U.S. enjoyed from the international monetary order it crafted at the Bretton Woods conference of 1944. The Russian and Chinese governments have not yet awoken to the geo-strategic benefits of Bitcoin as a reserve currency and are currently preoccupied with the effects it may have on their internal markets. Like de Gaulle in the 1960s, who threatened to reestablish the classical gold standard in response to the US's exorbitant privilege, the Chinese and Russians will, in time, come to see the benefits of a large reserve position in a nonsovereign store of value. With the largest concentration of Bitcoin mining power residing in China, the Chinese state already has a distinct advantage in its potential to add bitcoins to its reserves.

The United States prides itself as a nation of innovators, with Silicon Valley being a crown jewel in the U.S. economy. Thus far, Silicon Valley has largely dominated the conversation on the position that regulators should take vis-à-vis Bitcoin. However, the banking industry and the U.S. Federal Reserve are finally having their first inkling of the existential threat Bitcoin poses to U.S. monetary policy if it were to become a global reserve currency. The *Wall Street Journal*, known to be a mouthpiece for the Federal Reserve, published a commentary on the threat Bitcoin poses to U.S. monetary policy:

> There is another danger, perhaps even more serious from the point of view of the central banks and regulators: bitcoin might not crash. If the speculative fervor in the cryptocurrency is merely the precursor to it being widely used as an alternative to the dollar, it will threaten the central banks' monopoly on money.[26]

In the coming years, there will be a great struggle between entrepreneurs and innovators, on the one hand, who will attempt to keep Bitcoin free of regulatory control,

26   http://bullishcaseforbitcoin.com/references/wsj-quote

and the banking industry and central banks, on the other, who will use their influence to promote Bitcoin regulations in order to prevent disruption of their industry and money-issuing powers.

THE TRANSITION TO A MEDIUM OF EXCHANGE

A monetary good cannot transition to being a generally accepted medium of exchange (the standard economic definition of money) before it is widely valued, for the tautological reason that a good that is not valued will not be accepted in exchange. In the process of becoming widely valued, and hence a store of value, a monetary good will soar in purchasing power, creating an opportunity cost to relinquishing it for use in exchange. Only when the opportunity cost of relinquishing a store of value drops to a suitably low level can it transition to becoming a generally accepted medium of exchange.

More precisely, a monetary good will only be suitable as a medium of exchange when the sum of the opportunity cost and the transactional cost of using it in exchange drops below the cost of trading without it.

In a barter-based society, the transition of a store of value to a medium of exchange can occur even when the monetary good is increasing in purchasing power because the transactional costs of barter trade are extremely high. In a developed economy, where transactional costs are low, it is possible for a nascent and rapidly appreciating store of value, such as Bitcoin, to be used as a medium of exchange, albeit within a limited scope. An example is the illicit drug market, where buyers are willing to sacrifice the opportunity of holding bitcoins to minimize the substantial risk of purchasing the drugs using fiat currency.

There are, however, major institutional barriers to a nascent store of value becoming a *generally* accepted medium of exchange in a developed society. States use taxation as a powerful means to protect their sovereign money from being displaced by competing monetary goods. Not only does a sovereign money enjoy the advantage of a constant source of demand, by way of taxes being remittable only in that form, but competing monetary goods are taxed whenever they are exchanged at an appreciated value. This latter kind of taxation creates significant friction to using a store of value as a medium of exchange.

The handicapping of market-based monetary goods is not an insurmountable barrier to their adoption as a generally accepted medium of exchange, however. If faith is lost in a sovereign money, its value can collapse in a process known as hyperinflation. When a sovereign money hyperinflates, its value first collapses against the most liquid goods in the society such as gold or foreign money like the U.S. dollar, if they are available. When no liquid goods are available or their supply is limited, a hyperinflating money collapses against real goods, such as real estate and commodities. The archetypal image of a hyperinflation is a grocery store emptied of all its produce as consumers flee the rapidly diminishing value of their nation's money.

Eventually, when faith is completely lost during a hyperinflation, a sovereign money will no longer be accepted by anyone, and the society will either devolve to barter or the monetary unit will be completely replaced as a medium of exchange. An example of this process was the replacement of the Zimbabwe dollar with the U.S. dollar. The replacement of a sovereign money with a foreign one is made more difficult by the scarcity of the foreign money and the absence of foreign banking institutions to provide liquidity.

The ability to easily transmit bitcoins across borders and the absence of a need for a banking system make Bitcoin an ideal monetary good for those afflicted by hyperinflation. In the coming years, as fiat monies continue to follow their historical trend toward eventual worthlessness, Bitcoin will become an increasingly popular choice for global savings to flee to. When a nation's money is abandoned and replaced by Bitcoin, Bitcoin will have transitioned from being a store of value in that society to a generally accepted medium of exchange. Daniel Krawisz coined the term hyperbitcoinization to describe this process.[27]

27   http://bullishcaseforbitcoin.com/references/hyperbitcoinization

CHAPTER 5

A NEW MONETARY BASE

COMMON MISCONCEPTIONS

MUCH OF THIS BOOK HAS FOCUSED ON THE MONETARY nature of Bitcoin. With this foundation, we can now address the most common misconceptions about this revolutionary monetary good.

IS BITCOIN A BUBBLE?

Bitcoin has a monetary premium that gives rise to the common criticism that Bitcoin is a bubble. However, *all* monetary goods have a monetary premium. Indeed, it is this premium (the excess over the use-demand price) that is the defining characteristic of all monies. Thus, in a sense, money can be said to always and everywhere be a bubble. Paradoxically, a monetary good is both a bubble and may be *undervalued* if it is in the early stages of its adoption for use as money.

IS BITCOIN TOO VOLATILE TO BE A STORE OF VALUE?

Bitcoin's price volatility is a function of its nascency. In the first few years of its existence, Bitcoin behaved like a penny stock, and any large buyer, such as the Winklevoss twins, could cause a large spike in its price. As adoption and liquidity have increased over the years, Bitcoin's volatility has decreased commensurately. When Bitcoin achieves the market capitalization of gold, it should display a similar level of volatility. As Bitcoin surpasses the market capitalization of gold, its volatility will decrease to a level that will make it suitable as a widely used medium of exchange. As previously noted, the monetization of Bitcoin occurs in a series of Gartner hype cycles. Volatility is lowest during the plateau phase of the hype cycle and highest during the peak and crash phases of the cycle. Each hype cycle has lower volatility than previous cycles because the liquidity of the market has increased.

IS BITCOIN TOO EXPENSIVE TO INVEST IN?

A common complaint among investors new to the Bitcoin market is that an individual bitcoin is too expensive to purchase. This complaint is often a result of the mistaken belief that bitcoins can only be purchased in whole units rather than in smaller fractions. In fact, the divisibility of Bitcoin allows investors to purchase trifling sums of the currency, such as a single dollar's worth. In other instances, the desire to own a whole bitcoin is the result of a human psychological tendency known as unit bias. Unit bias is the desire to complete a task or fulfill some objective in its entirety, and research has shown it is a potential factor in the human proclivity to overeat.[28]

The desire to own a whole unit of a cryptocurrency leads many investors to mistakenly believe that competing cryptocurrencies are more affordable because individual units of those currencies have a lower price. However, the cheaper unit price of many of Bitcoin's competitors is due to their much higher unit supply, which is arbitrarily chosen and not in itself indicative of the value of the currency. Investors should not focus on the price of an individual unit, but rather on the market capitalization and liquidity of the whole currency; the much larger capitalization and significantly deeper liquidity of Bitcoin is a reflection of its stronger network effect and utility for storing value.

An associated apprehension is that most of Bitcoin's financial returns are in the past rather than in the future, due to its previous meteoric rise, leaving many new investors with a sense that they have missed out. While it is true that the earliest owners of an economic good in the process of monetization will see the greatest financial gains

28   http://bullishcaseforbitcoin.com/references/unit-bias

(assuming they are able to hold over the long term) this does not imply that latecomers will not enjoy good returns. The rate of financial returns will diminish over time as the pool of savings entering a new monetary good slows and eventually dwindles. But for Bitcoin, the addressable market encompasses the entire market for storing value, which amounts to hundreds of trillions of dollars in value and includes the gold market, government bonds, real estate, and fine art. Bitcoin clearly has not reached full market saturation. Even in an outcome where Bitcoin becomes the world's reserve currency and the inflow of savings to it stabilizes, owners will still see financial returns proportional to the productivity of the global economy in which it has become the unit of account.

ARE TRANSACTION FEES TOO HIGH?

A recent criticism of the Bitcoin network is that the increase in fees to transmit bitcoins makes it unsuitable as a payment system. However, the growth in fees is healthy and expected. Transaction fees are a cost required to pay bitcoin miners to secure the network by validating transactions. Miners are compensated by the sum of transaction fees plus the block subsidy, which is an inflationary payout borne by current bitcoin owners.

Given Bitcoin's fixed supply schedule—a monetary policy that makes it an ideal store of value—the block subsidy will eventually decline to zero, and the network must ultimately be secured with transaction fees. A network with "low" fees is a network with little security and one prone to external censorship. Those touting the low fees of Bitcoin alternatives are unknowingly describing the weakness of these so-called alt-coins.

The specious root of the criticism of Bitcoin's "high" transaction fees is the belief that Bitcoin should be a payment system first and a store of value later. As we have seen with the origins of money, this belief puts the cart before the horse. Only when Bitcoin has become a deeply established store of value will it become suitable as a medium of exchange. Furthermore, once the opportunity cost of trading bitcoins reaches a level at which it is suitable for use as a medium of exchange, most trades will not occur on the Bitcoin network itself, but rather on second-layer networks with much lower fees. A second-layer network allows parties to exchange bitcoins off-chain—that is, without broadcasting every transaction to the Bitcoin network—with final settlement eventually occurring on the blockchain. The use of a second-layer network facilitates a much higher volume of cheap, fast transactions than would be possible on-chain.

Second-layer networks, such as the Lightning network, provide the modern equivalent of the promissory notes that were used to transfer titles for gold in the nineteenth century. Promissory notes were used by banks because transferring the underlying bullion was far more costly than transferring a note representing the title to the gold. Unlike promissory notes, however, the Lightning network will allow the transfer of bitcoins at low cost while requiring little or no trust of third parties such as banks. The development of the Lightning network is a profoundly important technical innovation in Bitcoin's history, and its value will become apparent as it is developed and adopted in the coming years.

DOES BITCOIN CONSUME TOO MUCH ELECTRICITY?

The energy expenditure of Bitcoin's network, required for the purpose of mining, has been a cause of criticism among many anti-Bitcoin activists who fault the potentially negative impact it may have on the Earth's environment. A common refrain is that Bitcoin's network consumes more electricity than some small nation, implying that this is an indictment of Bitcoin in and of itself. According to the Cambridge Center for Alternative Finance, at the time of writing, Bitcoin's network consumes approximately 105 terawatt-hours of energy annually. Concerned investors may legitimately question whether societies will tolerate such a significant expenditure in the future and whether this may pose a political threat to Bitcoin's continued existence.

Policy-makers and investors must go beyond tendentious sound-bites when performing a critical analysis of Bitcoin's energy consumption. Nuances that should be considered in an impartial analysis include the source of Bitcoin's energy consumption and whether it is environmentally harmful, whether the energy consumed displaces other uses and, most importantly, the utility provided to society made possible by such energy usage. In this section, I will endeavor to consider these nuances through a comparative analysis of Bitcoin with its main competitors. As a system for storing and transmitting value, Bitcoin's nearest competitors are gold and the various fiat monetary systems used globally.

A 2014 survey of peer-reviewed studies on the environmental impact of gold mining by Hass McCook concluded that the annual energy expenditure of gold production was approximately 475 gigajoules or 132 terrawatt-hours.[29]

The environmental effects of gold mining are harsh and obvious

Although it superficially appears that the energy consumption of Bitcoin and gold are similar, the environmental impact of gold mining greatly exceeds that of its Bitcoin counterpart. A study published in the *International Journal*

29   http://bullishcaseforbitcoin.com/references/mccook-article

A Bitcoin mining farm

of Environmental Research and Public Health by Fashola et al. explains that "[gold] mining activities can lead to the generation of large quantities of heavy metal-laden wastes which are released in an uncontrolled manner, causing widespread contamination of the ecosystem."[30] In contrast, Bitcoin mining only requires the operation of computers on which Bitcoin's mining software runs, often housed in large data centers similar to those used by Google, Facebook, and Microsoft. Furthermore, unlike gold mining, which must take place near the source of the gold ore being mined, Bitcoin mining can take place in any location where there is a power source and an Internet connection. Combined with the ease and cheapness with which bitcoins can be transmitted, Bitcoin mining gravitates toward sources of power that are overbuilt and produce excess electricity that would

30   http://bullishcaseforbitcoin.com/references/gold-mining-impact

otherwise go to waste. A prominent example of overbuilt electrical capacity is the hydroelectric dams in Sichuan province in China, one of the largest centers of Bitcoin mining. David Stanway, a senior correspondent for industry and environment at *Thomson Reuters*, explains that "Sichuan underlines the case. Total hydropower reached more than 75 GW in 2017, greater than the total in most Asian countries. It was also more than double the capacity of the province's power grid, meaning lots of wasted power."[31]

Given that excess energy can only be transported limited distances, due to decay over power lines, Bitcoin mining essentially rescues wasted energy and transforms it into a digital good that can be easily transmitted around the world. In this way, Bitcoin mining can be thought of as a means of unlocking stranded energy that would be otherwise uneconomical to produce or would go to waste due to limited usage in its geographical location. Furthermore, many sources of excess energy are renewable in nature and do not meaningfully contribute to global carbon emissions. Examples include the aforementioned use of hydroelectric energy in China and geothermal energy used by Bitcoin mining facilities in Iceland. Thus, Bitcoin can be viewed as a force for environmental good by making renewable energy producers more profitable and increasing the incentive for investment in future production. A 2019 study by CoinShares Research concluded that "a conservative estimate of the renewables penetration in the energy mix

31   http://bullishcaseforbitcoin.com/references/hydro-article

powering the Bitcoin mining network [is] 74.1%, making Bitcoin mining more renewables-driven than almost every other large-scale industry in the world."[32]

When comparing the environmental cost of Bitcoin mining to fiat monetary systems, one must recognize that it is not simply the financial infrastructure that should be accounted for, but also the political cost that gives the monetary system enough credibility that a citizenry would place their trust in it. History is littered with examples of nation-states whose money and monetary systems collapsed when they were conquered or splintered into factions. Without a military to enforce geographical boundaries and a police force to enforce property rights, no sovereign monetary system could survive. It is here that Bitcoin truly excels. Where sovereign monies require an apparatus of coercion to exist (i.e., the state), Bitcoin provides the foundation for a new monetary system where property rights do not need to be maintained by a sovereign. An individual who owns bitcoins can be thought of as having a "super property right": ownership in a valuable good that can easily be held and transmitted without the support or sanction of the state.

Ultimately, the energy consumed by the Bitcoin network will be proportional to the demand from the world's citizenry to use a permissionless system for savings and exchange and the utility that system affords them. As Satoshi Nakamoto explained, "[t]he utility of the exchanges made possible by Bitcoin will far exceed the cost of

32   http://bullishcaseforbitcoin.com/references/coinshares-paper-1

electricity used. Therefore, not having Bitcoin would be the net waste."[33]

For those living under oppressive regimes, Bitcoin's utility is more than theoretical and may be a matter of life and death. In a New York Times opinion piece, Venezuelan economist Carlos Hernández explained that owning Bitcoin allowed him to weather the ravages of hyperinflation and allowed his brother to escape Venezuela without having his savings confiscated.

> Venezuelan military personnel at the borders have a reputation for seizing the money of people who want to leave, but Juan's, being in Bitcoin, was accessible only with a password he had memorized. "Borderless money" is more than a buzzword for those of us who live in a collapsing economy and a collapsing dictatorship.[34]

WILL BITCOIN BE OVERTAKEN BY A COMPETING CRYPTOCURRENCY?

As an open-source software protocol, it has always been possible to copy Bitcoin's software and imitate its network. Over the years, many imitators have been created, ranging from ersatz facsimiles such as Litecoin to complex variants like Ethereum that promise to allow arbitrarily complex contractual arrangements using a distributed

---

33   http://bullishcaseforbitcoin.com/references/satoshi-electricity-quote

34   http://bullishcaseforbitcoin.com/references/venezuela-story

computational system. A common criticism of Bitcoin is that it cannot maintain its value when competitors are easy to create and are able to incorporate the latest innovations and software features.

The fallacy in this argument is the assumption that cryptocurrencies compete on their technological attributes; rather, they compete on their *monetary* attributes. Technology has value only insofar as it gives credibility to the monetary attributes of a cryptocurrency, such as scarcity. In this sense, boring, well-tested, and stable technology is preferable to cutting-edge innovation.

Furthermore, the scores of Bitcoin competitors that have been created over the years lack the network effect of the first and dominant technology in the space. A network effect—the increased value of using Bitcoin simply because it is already the dominant network—is a feature in and of itself. For any technology that possesses a network effect, it is by far the most important feature.

The network effect for Bitcoin encompasses the liquidity of its market, the number of people who own it and the community of developers maintaining and improving its software and brand awareness. Large investors, including nation-states, will seek the most liquid market so that they can enter and exit the market quickly without affecting its price. Developers will flock to the dominant development community that has the highest-caliber talent, thereby reinforcing the strength of that community. Also, brand awareness is self-reinforcing; would-be competitors to Bitcoin are always mentioned in the context of Bitcoin itself.

ARE FORKS A THREAT TO BITCOIN?

A trend that became popular in 2017 was not only to imitate Bitcoin's software, but also to copy the entire history of its past transactions (the blockchain). By copying Bitcoin's blockchain up to a certain point and then splitting off into a new network, in a process known as forking, competitors of Bitcoin were able to solve the problem of distributing their tokens to a large user base.

The most significant fork of this kind occurred on August 1, 2017, when a new network known as Bitcoin Cash (BCash) was created. An owner of N bitcoins before August 1, 2017 would then own both N bitcoins and N BCash tokens. The small but vocal community of BCash proponents tirelessly attempted to expropriate Bitcoin's brand recognition,

A fork in the road

both through the deceptive naming of their new network and a campaign to convince neophytes in the Bitcoin market that BCash was the "real" Bitcoin. These attempts failed, and this failure is reflected in the relatively minuscule market capitalization of the BCash network. However, for new investors, there remains an apparent risk that a competitor might clone Bitcoin and its blockchain and succeed in overtaking it in market capitalization, thus becoming the de facto Bitcoin.

An important rule can be gleaned from the major forks that occurred with both the Bitcoin and Ethereum networks. Most of the market capitalization will settle on the network that retains the highest-caliber and most active developer community. Although Bitcoin can be viewed as a nascent form of money, it is also a computer network built on software that needs to be maintained and improved. Buying tokens on a network with little or inexperienced developer support would be akin to buying a clone of Microsoft Windows that was not supported by Microsoft's best developers. It is clear from the history of the forks that occurred in 2017 that the best and most experienced computer scientists and cryptographers are committed to developing the original Bitcoin and not any of the growing legion of imitators that have been created from it.

IS BITCOIN REALLY SCARCE?

While the supply of bitcoins within the Bitcoin network is limited to no more than 21 million, some have contended that because Bitcoin's software can easily be copied and its blockchain forked, the creation of new tokens on several copycat networks implies that Bitcoin's scarcity is illusory. By this flawed logic, each copy made of the Mona Lisa dilutes the singularity of the original. Rather, each copy of Da Vinci's masterpiece just serves to illustrate that there is only one *real* Mona Lisa. Similarly, each copy made of Bitcoin illustrates that there is only one network with a dominant network effect, brand recognition, and monetary scale that allows billions of dollars in value to be transferred each day.

REAL RISKS

Although the common criticisms of Bitcoin are misplaced and based on a flawed understanding of money, there are real and significant risks to investing in Bitcoin. It would be prudent for a prospective Bitcoin investor to understand and weigh these risks when considering an investment in Bitcoin.

PROTOCOL RISK

The Bitcoin protocol and the cryptographic primitives on which it is built could be found to have a design flaw or could be made insecure with the development of quantum computing. If a flaw is found in the protocol or if some new means of computation breaks the cryptography underpinning Bitcoin, faith in Bitcoin as a store of value may be severely compromised. Protocol risk was highest in the early years of Bitcoin's development when it was still unclear, even to seasoned cryptographers, that Satoshi Nakamoto had truly found a solution to the Byzantine Generals Problem. Concerns about serious flaws in the Bitcoin protocol have dissipated over the years as numerous attempts to break it have failed and real flaws have been found and fixed. Furthermore, protocol developers have been aware of the risk of quantum computing for years and have researched potential solutions if the use of such computers becomes feasible.[35] However, given the technological nature of Bitcoin, protocol risk will always remain, if only as an outlier risk.

THE RISK OF STATE ATTACK

The threat of a state attack has hung over Bitcoin like a baleful pall since early in its history and it remains the gravest and most present risk that investors should weigh today. In a post to the Bitcointalk forum in December 2010, Satoshi Nakamoto fretted that Wikileaks, a website known

---

35   http://bullishcaseforbitcoin.com/references/quantum-computing

for publishing state secrets, was considering collecting donations using Bitcoin. Nakamoto explained that the attention brought by Wikileaks' potential usage of Bitcoin was unwanted because the embryonic system he had created was not yet resilient enough to withstand a concerted state attack. Nevertheless, the decentralized and permissionless nature of Bitcoin attracted usage for proscribed purposes early on, including the drug marketplace Silk Road that opened in February 2011. It was Silk Road that first drew the attention of members of the U.S. Congress to Bitcoin, including West Virginia Senator Joe Manchin, who publicly appealed to Federal regulators to ban Bitcoin in 2014, writing:

> Due to Bitcoin's anonymity, the virtual market has been extremely susceptible to hackers and scam artists stealing millions from Bitcoins users. Anonymity combined with Bitcoin's ability to finalize transactions quickly, makes it very difficult, if not impossible, to reverse fraudulent transactions.
>
> Bitcoin has also become a haven for individuals to buy black market items. Individuals are able to anonymously purchase items such as drugs and weapons illegally. I have already written to regulators once on the now-closed Silkroad, which operated for years in supplying drugs and other black market items to criminals, thanks in large part to the creation of Bitcoin.[36]

36   http://bullishcaseforbitcoin.com/references/manchin-letter

Manchin mistakenly believed that Bitcoin was ideally suited for illicit trade because it was anonymous. In reality, Bitcoin's blockchain is public and open, allowing law enforcement agencies to employ blockchain analytics software to trace transactions years after they have taken place. The development of blockchain analytics and its employment in prosecuting several prominent criminal cases has muted the charge that Bitcoin is anonymous and is predominantly used for criminal activities. Over the years it has become apparent that the overwhelming source of demand for Bitcoin is as a means for savings and investment rather than for illicit trade. Yet it is precisely Bitcoin's usage as a store of value that undermines a key sovereign power of any nation-state: control over the nation's money. The concern for loss of control over monetary policy will provide continuing motivation for many states to contemplate an attack on Bitcoin.

A state attack on Bitcoin could take many forms ranging from onerous regulation of its usage, such as forcing users to report the identity of the recipient of sent bitcoins prior to sending them, to making mere ownership criminal or even attempting confiscation. While the threat of confiscation may seem far-fetched, there are precedents for states attacking the property rights of their citizens in this way. In 1933, President Franklin Roosevelt, ostensibly attempting to mitigate the Great Depression, issued Executive Order 6102, ordering U.S. citizens to relinquish their gold and making its ownership illegal. Due to the difficulty of transporting, securing, and assaying gold, there was a tendency for owners of it to keep their holdings with financial institutions, creating a more centralized and coercible target for the U.S. government.

Executive Order 6102

In contrast, being digital and decentralized in design, Bitcoin has shown a remarkable degree of resilience in the face of numerous attempts by various governments to regulate or ban its use. However, the exchanges where bitcoins are traded for fiat currencies are highly centralized and susceptible to regulation and closure. Without these exchanges and the willingness of the banking system to do business with them, the process of monetization of Bitcoin would be severely stunted, if not halted completely. While there are alternative sources of liquidity for Bitcoin, such as over-the-counter brokers and decentralized markets for buying and selling bitcoins, the critical process of price discovery happens on the most liquid exchanges, which are all centralized.

Mitigating the risk of exchange shutdowns is jurisdictional arbitrage. Binance, a prominent exchange that started in China, moved its headquarters to Japan and then Malta after the Chinese government halted its mainland operations. National governments are also wary of smothering a nascent industry that may prove as consequential as the Internet, thereby ceding a tremendous competitive advantage to other nations.

Only with a coordinated global shutdown of Bitcoin exchanges would the process of monetization be halted completely. The race is on for Bitcoin to become so widely adopted that a complete shutdown becomes as politically infeasible as a complete shutdown of the Internet. One hopeful sign is the increasing adoption of Bitcoin among financial institutions and corporations, both of which are generally more adept at lobbying governments than retail investors. Furthermore, the largest U.S. exchange, Coinbase, recently listed as a public company commanding a valuation of 100 billion dollars at the time of writing. Policy-makers are likely to be cautious when enacting policies that could destroy billions of dollars of market capitalization and potentially harm millions of retail investors. Finally, the process of political capture, whereby politicians and their constituents have an increased ideological affinity for Bitcoin simply because they own it, is steadily increasing and provides a natural bulwark against hostile policies.

The possibility of a global shutdown of exchanges is still real, however, and must be factored into the risks of investing in Bitcoin. As was discussed in Chapter 4, national governments are finally awakening to the threat that a non-sovereign, censorship-resistant digital currency poses to their monetary policies. It is an open question whether they will act on this threat before Bitcoin becomes so entrenched that political action against it proves ineffectual.

THE RISK OF MINER CENTRALIZATION

Bitcoin miners are computers on the Bitcoin network that serve the purpose of validating and establishing a temporal ordering of transactions submitted to the network. An important risk that investors should consider is the possibility that the computational resources devoted to Bitcoin mining, referred to as hash power, become too centralized.

If control of the hash power of the network were concentrated in too few hands, it might become possible to attack the network, either politically or economically in a process known as double spending.

Double spending occurs when a mining firm or cartel with a majority of the total hash power exchanges bitcoins for something valuable, such as dollars, and then uses their mining resources to reorganize the blockchain so that the original transfer never occurred. Double spending is a costly endeavor fraught with risk; the reorganization of the blockchain is not guaranteed to succeed and, even if it did, a successful purloining would undermine confidence in Bitcoin itself so that the attacker would be harming their own savings. Satoshi Nakamoto anticipated the threat of double spending from the very beginning, observing in his original whitepaper that Bitcoin was designed in such a way that potential attackers had a greater incentive to mine honestly than to double spend:

> If a greedy attacker is able to assemble more CPU power than all the honest nodes, he would have to choose between using it to defraud people by stealing back his payments, or using it to generate new coins. He ought to find it more profitable to play by the rules, such rules that favour him with more new coins than everyone else combined, than to undermine the system and the validity of his own wealth.

When first published in 2008, before Bitcoin's network even existed, Nakamoto's claim was still only a theoretical contention and based on the assumption that attackers were economically rational. Recent research by Savolainen and Ruiz-Ogarrio has corroborated Nakamoto's claim in practice:

> We conclude that the historically observed [mining] pool concentration does not indicate a higher risk of double spending attacks. ... Hence, our result directly contradicts the common belief that concentration is harmful. This result demonstrates the well-known economic insight that feasibility does not imply desirability.[37]

While Nakamoto's original design of Bitcoin anticipated the possibility of double spending under the assumption of economically rational agents, it did not account for a concerted political attack on mining firms by a nation-state with non-economic ends. Nation-states have often acted in economically irrational ways to further their political ends, such as waging war on their neighbors. A nation-state might be motivated to carry out a political attack on Bitcoin mining to prevent its citizenry from availing itself of a means of saving and transacting outside the state's jurisdiction. Alternatively, a nation-state may desire Bitcoin's demise because of a belief that it poses a systemic threat to

---

37   http://bullishcaseforbitcoin.com/references/too-big-to-cheat-paper

the state's monetary policy. If a nation-state were to appropriate enough of the computing resources used for Bitcoin mining, it could potentially censor transactions that it did not approve of, or simply deprive the network of that hash power, dramatically reducing network security and undermining confidence in the currency itself.

Of the nation-states with a motivation to attack Bitcoin's network, the People's Republic of China currently has the greatest capability. Due to its dominance of chip fabrication and the overcapacity of energy production in some of its provinces, China has become the global center for production of mining hardware and the home of the largest mining operations. A 2019 study by CoinShares Research estimated that "as much as 65% of Bitcoin hash power resides within China."[38] If the Chinese state were to nationalize the companies producing mining hardware and those doing the mining itself, it could pose a significant threat to the operation of Bitcoin's network. Although there is no way to eliminate the risk of the Chinese state targeting Bitcoin, there is a nuclear option that could neutralize an attack in the event it occurred: altering Bitcoin's proof-of-work function. Before we can fully understand this nuclear option, we must briefly explore the history of Bitcoin mining.

Since the inception of Bitcoin's network in 2009, the computers used for mining have become increasingly specialized to maximize the hash power generated per unit of

---

38   http://bullishcaseforbitcoin.com/references/coinshares-paper-2

electricity consumed. In the earliest days, participants in the network used their regular computers for mining, but by May 2010 Lazslo Hanyecz had discovered that computer chips optimized for image processing, known as GPUs, were far more efficient at mining than regular CPUs. Hanyecz's discovery triggered an arms race in the development of mining hardware that ultimately led to the creation of application-specific integrated circuits (ASICs) for Bitcoin mining. The first ASIC miners were created in 2013 by China-based hardware manufacturer Canaan Creative, and since then several other chip manufacturers such as Bitmain and Bitfury have entered the highly competitive space. ASIC miners are computers developed to do one and only one thing with the utmost efficiency: run Bitcoin's proof-of-work function, known as SHA256, as rapidly as possible. By applying the SHA256 function exhaustively, a miner can find an acceptable hash required to create the next block on the blockchain, thereby collecting the block subsidy associated with it.

SHA256 is the fundamental building block of Bitcoin mining, and billions of dollars have been spent in the research and production of hardware that is optimized to run it. However, it is possible for SHA256 to be replaced as Bitcoin's proof-of-work function with an alternative, such as SHA512. Replacing Bitcoin's proof-of-work function would instantly render obsolete the mining hardware optimized to run SHA256, devastating the companies that produce it and the mining facilities that employ that hardware.

Such an extreme measure could potentially be used if Bitcoin mining were to come under attack by the Chinese state, but it would be extremely perilous. Without an overwhelming consensus of participants in the Bitcoin network and the investors who hold bitcoins as savings, changing the proof-of-work function could cause a fracturing of the network and splintering of the community into factions, each claiming that the network running their preferred proof-of-work function was the real Bitcoin. Furthermore, without the significant capital expenditure devoted to SHA256-based mining hardware and facilities, Bitcoin's network security would be dramatically lower until equivalent expenditures were made for the alternative proof-of-work function. Thus, a change of Bitcoin's proof-of-work function should rightly be considered a nuclear option only to be deployed in the gravest circumstances. Even if never deployed, the threat that Bitcoin's proof-of-work function *could* be changed is a powerful check on any nation-state hoping to appropriate Bitcoin's hash power for its own ends.

CUSTODIAL RISK

Corporate and institutional buyers of Bitcoin often rely on regulated custodians when storing their bitcoins. As its value continues to rise, hundreds of billions of dollars' worth of Bitcoin will be in the care of these custodians, presenting an increasingly attractive target for hackers. Where custodians for physical gold only need to contend with potential security threats that are proximate to the location of the stored gold, custodians of Bitcoin must contend with hackers that can target custodied funds from anywhere on Earth. A successful heist of a major regulated Bitcoin custodian may severely damage confidence among corporate and institutional investors.

Mitigating the threat of a major hacking attack are improvements in security practices across the entire industry and the development of tools for managing funds without ever needing those funds to be accessible to the Internet. While a major theft can never be fully ruled out, it appears that the likelihood of a catastrophic heist, such as the one that felled the first major Bitcoin exchange MtGox, is much lower than it was in Bitcoin's early history.

THE RISK OF FEDERAL RESERVE POLICY

During the late 1970s, the United States experienced a period of high monetary inflation that helped trigger a bull market in gold. The decade culminated in a crisis of confidence in the U.S. dollar that was only resolved by the drastic actions of the Federal Reserve Chairman, Paul Volcker, who was newly confirmed at the time. Volcker dramatically raised short-term interest rates to an unprecedented 20 percent in 1980, which threw the U.S. economy into a deep recession and sent gold into a multi-decade bear market, but also tamed the rampant price inflation of the 1970s.[39]

As a monetary good with trillions in market capitalization, gold was vulnerable to Federal Reserve policy. If the

---

39   http://bullishcaseforbitcoin.com/references/volcker-inflation-fighting

Portrait of former Federal Reserve Chairman, Paul Volcker

Federal Reserve drives interest rates high enough, the demand for gold, which has no natural yield, transfers to dollars that can collect interest at the Federal Reserve's short-term interest rate. Due to its smaller size, Bitcoin's price movements have largely been dictated by the flow of new investors into its market, but as Bitcoin approaches the same market capitalization as gold, it too will face macro-economic risks from Federal Reserve policy. If the Federal Reserve Board were to perceive a threat to the dollar's credibility from the continued monetization of Bitcoin, it could attempt to thwart that process by increasing interest rates steeply, as Volcker did in the early 1980s. Hindering such an effort, however, is the starkly different fiscal situation of the United States today in comparison to the late 1970s. Not since the debt incurred during the Second World War did the United States hold a debt position greater than 100 percent of its GDP, as it does now. In comparison, the debt-to-GDP ratio in 1980 was less than 40 percent. Thus, while the threat of Federal Reserve interest rate hikes exists, it would be difficult for the U.S. central bank to pursue such a policy without making it much more onerous for the U.S. Treasury to service its outstanding debt; pursuing an aggressive interest rate policy in the current fiscal environment could potentially trigger a sovereign debt crisis. Thus, the Federal Reserve may be bound by fiscal factors to continue a policy that is favorable to Bitcoin's monetization, even as it approaches and surpasses gold in size.

THE RISK OF REHYPOTHECATION

Financial institutions that provide advanced investment products, such as shorting, buying on margin or derivatives, typically require their clients to provide collateral in the form of cash, stocks, bonds or other assets before they are given access to these products. Collateral is used as a means of mitigating risk when a client makes an imprudent investment that results in a loss. For example, if a client of a brokerage firm shorts a stock and the later stock increases in value, the brokerage can sell all or part of the client's collateral to cover the loss.

Rehypothecation is the practice whereby a financial institution uses the collateral provided to it for its own investment purposes, thereby potentially increasing its profits but also putting its clients' collateral at greater risk. In return for permitting their collateral to be invested or lent out, a client is compensated in some way, such as a lower interest rate when shorting. When done prudently, rehypothecation can allow financial institutions to provide investment products at lower cost or even for free, and it can also deepen market liquidity. However, when done imprudently and when the practice is pervasive, rehypothecation can become a systemic risk to a financial system. When collateral is lent out repeatedly and passes through many financial institutions, a failed investment at one institution can cause a series of cascading liquidations among many institutions, driving the price of the collateral asset down precipitously and triggering a liquidity crisis. Indeed, as Singh and Aitken argue in their 2010 IMF working paper, rehypothecation played an important role in the 2008 financial crisis: "Incorporating estimates for rehypothecation (and the associated re-use of collateral) in the recent crisis indicates that the collapse in non-bank funding to banks was sizable."[40]

Bitcoin's first significant use as a collateral asset came in 2014 with the founding of a Hong Kong-based cryptocurrency exchange, BitMex. BitMex's clients could deposit bitcoins on the exchange and then make bets on various derivative contracts, such as the Perpetual Swap contract. The contracts offered by BitMex created a way for its clients to bet on the future price of Bitcoin and to do so with

40   http://bullishcaseforbitcoin.com/references/imf-rehypothecation-article

leverage. By providing an exchange that did not require deposits in fiat currency, BitMex was able to circumvent the bureaucracies that typically regulate such markets, such as the CFTC, allowing the company to rapidly grow its business. By August 2020, the exchange was doing a staggering 75 billion dollars in trading volume, turning its co-founders into billionaires.[41] BitMex's pioneering use of Bitcoin as collateral and the financial success it enjoyed did not go unnoticed. Many businesses have since followed BitMex's lead, from the venerable Chicago Mercantile Exchange, which was founded in 1898 and now offers Bitcoin futures contracts, to BlockFi, which allows its clients to earn interest on their bitcoins. Market commentator Raoul Pal has called Bitcoin "pristine collateral" and there is indeed a growing recognition that it is an ideal form of collateral due to its innate attributes and the nature of its market:

1. Bitcoin has a global and deeply liquid market with billions of dollars in volume trading every day.

2. Bitcoin's markets are continually open, unlike regular stock markets, allowing financial institutions to sell their Bitcoin collateral whenever they perceive an increased risk to their loan portfolio.

3. Bitcoins are not the obligation of any third party, unlike bonds, reducing counterparty risk.

---

41   http://bullishcaseforbitcoin.com/references/bitmex-story

4. Being digital, unlike gold, bitcoins are easy and inexpensive to take possession of, increasing the convenience of using Bitcoin as collateral.

With the growing recognition that Bitcoin is an ideal form of collateral, its increasing usage for this purpose will be a major source of demand in its monetization. Yet Bitcoin's growing use as a collateral asset brings an attendant risk of irresponsible rehypothecation. In an incipient industry, investors should rightly be wary of the quality of underwriting at the institutions that are accepting Bitcoin as collateral and subsequently investing it. The risks of Bitcoin rehypothecation are, perhaps, even greater than for other assets such as stocks and bonds. During a liquidity crisis, if many financial institutions are forced to sell bonds that have been taken as collateral, the collapse in prices will be protected by the cash flow of the bonds. Without cash flow to provide a safety net for its valuation, a liquidity crisis in Bitcoin could cause a disorderly collapse in its price. As we saw in the third chapter's discussion of the path-dependent nature of money, a collapse in Bitcoin's price could cause a significant shift in expectations about prospects for its future monetization, thereby stunting or even halting that process.

The greatest protections against the risk of rehypothecation are strong market regulation and industry transparency about the controls used to manage investments of collateral. Regulation is often taken to mean oversight by a regulatory body, such as the CFTC, but in practice such bureaucracies are slow to understand and satisfactorily supervise new and innovative industries, often relying on antiquated regulations conceived decades ago. By far the most important regulation is that of the market itself; institutions that invest irresponsibly should be allowed to fail, ensuring that poor practices are punished and will not become systemic in the industry, as they did during the housing crisis of 2008.

THE RISK OF IMPERFECT FUNGIBILITY

The open and transparent nature of the Bitcoin blockchain makes it possible for states to mark certain bitcoins as being tainted by their use in proscribed activities. Although Bitcoin's censorship resistance at the protocol level allows these bitcoins to be transmitted, if regulations were to appear that banned the use of such tainted bitcoins by exchanges or merchants, they could become largely worthless. Bitcoin would then lose one of the critical properties of a monetary good: fungibility.

To ameliorate Bitcoin's imperfect fungibility, improvements will need to be made at the protocol level to improve the privacy of transactions. While there are new developments in this regard, pioneered in digital currencies such as Monero and ZCash, there are major technological tradeoffs to be made between the efficiency and complexity of Bitcoin and its privacy. It remains an open question whether privacy-enhancing features can be added to

Bitcoin in a way that does not compromise its usefulness as money in other ways.

CONCLUSION

Bitcoin is an incipient money that is transitioning from the collectible stage of monetization to becoming a store of value. As a nonsovereign monetary good, it is possible that at some stage in the future Bitcoin will become a global reserve currency much like gold during the classical gold standard of the nineteenth century. The adoption of Bitcoin as a reserve currency is precisely the bullish case for Bitcoin and was articulated by Satoshi Nakamoto as early as 2010 in an email exchange with Mike Hearn: "If you imagine it being used for some fraction of world commerce, then there's only going to be 21 million coins for the whole world, so it would be worth much more per unit."[42]

This case was made even more trenchantly by the brilliant cryptographer Hal Finney, the recipient of the first bitcoins sent by Nakamoto, shortly after the announcement of the release of the first working Bitcoin software:

> [I]magine that Bitcoin is successful and becomes the dominant payment system in use throughout the world. Then the total value of the currency should be equal to the total value of all the wealth in the world. Current estimates of total worldwide household wealth that I have found range from

42   http://bullishcaseforbitcoin.com/references/satoshi-hearn-email

$100 trillion to $300 trillion. With 20 million coins, that gives each coin a value of about $10 million.[43]

Even if Bitcoin were not to become a fully-fledged reserve currency and were simply to compete with gold as a nonsovereign store of value, it is currently significantly undervalued. Mapping the market capitalization of the extant above-ground gold supply (approximately 10 trillion dollars) to the current mined supply of bitcoins gives a value of approximately $540,000 per bitcoin. As we have seen in Chapter 2, in terms of the attributes that make a monetary good suitable as a store of value, Bitcoin is either comparable or superior to gold for every criterion except for established history. As time passes and the Lindy effect takes hold, established history will no longer be a competitive advantage for gold. Thus, it is not unreasonable to expect that Bitcoin will approach and perhaps surpass gold's market capitalization in the next decade.

A caveat to this thesis is that a large fraction of gold's capitalization comes from central banks holding it as a store of value. For Bitcoin to achieve or surpass gold's capitalization, some participation by nation-states will be necessary. Whether the Western democracies will participate in the ownership of Bitcoin is unclear. It is more likely, unfortunately, that tin-pot dictatorships and kleptocracies will be the first nations to enter the Bitcoin market.

---

43   http://bullishcaseforbitcoin.com/references/hal-finney-quote

If no nation-states participate in the Bitcoin market, there still remains a bullish case for Bitcoin. As a nonsovereign store of value used only by retail and institutional investors, Bitcoin is still early in its adoption curve: the so-called early majority are now entering the market while the late majority and laggards are still years away from entering. With broader participation from retail and especially institutional investors, a price level between $100,000 and $250,000 is feasible.

Owning bitcoins is one of the few asymmetric bets that people across the entire world can participate in. Much like a call option, an investor's downside is limited to 1x, while their potential upside is still 100x or more. Bitcoin is the first truly global bubble whose size and scope are limited only by the desire of the world's citizenry to protect their savings from the vagaries of government economic mismanagement. Indeed, Bitcoin rose like a phoenix from the ashes of the 2008 global financial catastrophe—a catastrophe that was precipitated by the policies of central banks like the Federal Reserve.

Beyond the financial case for Bitcoin, its rise as a non-sovereign store of value will have profound geopolitical consequences. A global, noninflationary reserve currency will force nation-states to alter their primary funding mechanism from inflation to direct taxation, which is far less politically palatable. States will shrink in size commensurate to the political pain of transitioning to taxation as their exclusive means of funding. Furthermore, global trade will be settled in a manner that satisfies Charles de Gaulle's aspiration that no nation should have privilege over any other:

> We consider it necessary that international trade be established, as it was the case, before the great misfortunes of the World, on an indisputable monetary base, and one that does not bear the mark of any particular country.[44]

Fifty years from now, that monetary base will be Bitcoin.

---

44   http://bullishcaseforbitcoin.com/references/degaulle-speech

EPILOGUE

THE GREAT DEBATE

WHAT *IS* BITCOIN? THIS SEEMINGLY SIMPLE QUESTION AND the debate that arose to answer it roiled the community of Bitcoin developers and investors for several years, culminating in a schism in the community and a split of the Bitcoin network on August 1, 2017. In the years after Satoshi Nakamoto created Bitcoin, two main ideological factions emerged, each supporting a different vision for its future. The first faction saw Bitcoin primarily as a payment system akin to Visa or PayPal, but without a centralized point of control. They emphasized the transactional use of Bitcoin and believed that money is defined primarily by its role as a medium of exchange. The second faction stressed the importance of Bitcoin being uncensorable and warned of the dangers of ceding control of Bitcoin's protocol to any particular interest group. This faction envisioned Bitcoin as a digital version of gold, emphasizing its use as a nonsovereign store of value.

Complicating the contention between the two ideological factions was the disappearance of Bitcoin's creator not long after its creation. On December 12, 2010, 772 days after first appearing online to publish the design of Bitcoin, Satoshi Nakamoto made his final post to an online Bitcoin forum. Nakamoto's disappearance was of great consequence to the incipient software project that he had founded. Without its creator, the community of developers working on Bitcoin's software had to continue their work without guidance or a common future vision. One of the clearest statements we have of Nakamoto's aspirations for the project comes from his seminal publication, the "Bitcoin Whitepaper," published on October 31, 2008. Yet that short document fails to decisively answer the question of whether Bitcoin should be thought of first as a medium of exchange or as a store of value. Despite writing hundreds of forum posts and emails to the community of developers working on Bitcoin, Satoshi never unambiguously explained its monetary nature. In some of his writing, Nakamoto emphasized Bitcoin's similarity to gold and its use as a store of value:

> [Bitcoin is] more typical of a precious metal. Instead of the supply changing to keep the value the same, the supply is predetermined and the value changes. As the number of users grows, the value per coin increases. It has the potential for a positive feedback loop; as users increase, the value goes up, which could attract more users to take advantage of the increasing value.[45]

On several other occasions Nakamoto discussed Bitcoin for use in payments, emphasizing the medium-of-exchange role of money.

45   http://bullishcaseforbitcoin.com/references/satoshi-gold-quote

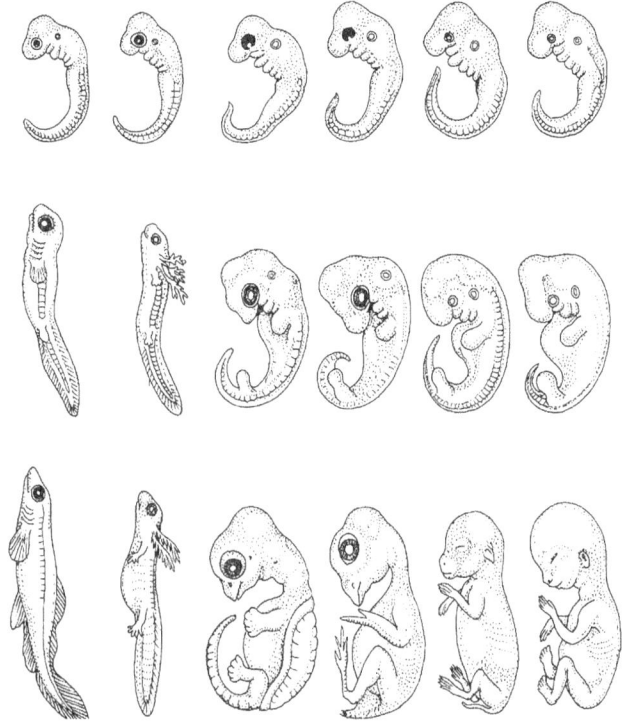

Embryos of different species appear alike

In its embryonic form, Bitcoin appeared to embody each vision with equal plausibility. On the one hand, Bitcoin's network began with low transaction fees, allowing bitcoins to be transferred at low cost around the world, seemingly providing a comparative advantage to alternative payments systems such as the Visa credit-card network. On the other hand, the exchange value of bitcoins increased significantly over time, suggesting it was a nascent store-of-value. But just as many species appear alike in their embryonic form, imprinted in their DNA are the instructions that will reveal their great differences in the fullness of time. Bitcoin's DNA lay in the consensus rules of its protocol and, as we shall see, these rules would make it clear that only one of these visions for Bitcoin would be realizable.

THE IMMUTABILITY OF PROTOCOLS

A protocol is a set of rules that participants in a system must abide by when using the system. Examples of software protocols include TCP/IP, which governs how data is encoded and transmitted across the Internet, and SMTP, which governs email-specific Internet traffic. Protocols can also apply to the physical world; for instance, the IEC 60906-2 and NEMA 5-15 standards for power sockets describe the shape of electrical plugs plus the voltage and amperage of the power conducted through the sockets.

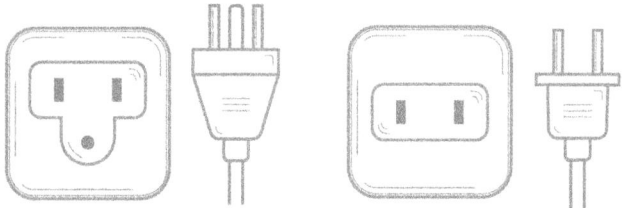

The ground slot is a backwards-compatible change to the original socket design

Protocols that are defined for use in software or hardware systems with many participants are usually very difficult to modify once in use, for good reason. Participants usually assume the immutability of a protocol when building businesses or devices that rely on it. Thus, changing a protocol for a widely used system would come at great cost to the ecosystem of participants who depend on it. Consider, for instance, the massive cost to North American households if the shape of power sockets were modified. Every socket in the nation would need to be updated, and every device that relied on the former socket shape would have to be discarded or provided with an adapter to use the new shape. An exception to the costliness of protocol updates are backwards-compatible changes that do not affect systems that use older versions of a protocol. For instance, the ground slot was invented in 1924 and provided a backwards-compatible update to sockets that reduced the risk of electrical shocks. Older devices with two-pronged electrical plugs were still able to use the newly designed sockets.

When Satoshi Nakamoto published the source code for Bitcoin on January 9, 2009, he had essentially produced a protocol for value transfer across the Internet. Nakamoto realized that once his design had come to life in a live, functioning network, it would be very difficult, if not impossible, to make non-backwards-compatible changes to the Bitcoin protocol. Commenting on this on June 17, 2010, Nakamoto observed that "Once version 0.1 was released, the core design was set in stone for the rest of its lifetime."[46]

---

46   http://bullishcaseforbitcoin.com/references/satoshi-protocol-quote

THE SCHISM

Bitcoin's protocol is defined by rules that specify which messages sent on the Bitcoin network are valid and these rules are enforced by computers on the network that run the Bitcoin software. Computers that do not abide by the so-called consensus rules are rejected from the network. Most famous among the consensus rules is the rule that determines how many new bitcoins may be minted per block. The block-subsidy rule defines Bitcoin's overall inflation schedule and limits the eventual total supply to no more than 21 million bitcoins. Another important rule is the maximum size of each block, which limits the total number of transactions that can be processed each time a new block is mined. This rule was originally created in 2010 as a means of hindering denial-of-service attacks to the budding network.[47]

Bitcoin's block-size rule was the main point of contention between the two factions debating the future of Bitcoin. One faction, referred to as big-blockers, wanted Bitcoin's protocol changed so that the block size was larger and could accommodate more transactions. Crucially, the proposed change would not be backwards-compatible and would cause a split in the network unless all network participants adopted it unanimously and at the same time. Big-blockers viewed Bitcoin as a piece of software, such as Microsoft Word, that should be upgraded frequently to satisfy the desires of businesses using it primarily for transactional purposes. The other faction, referred to as small-blockers,

---

47   http://bullishcaseforbitcoin.com/references/theymos-dos-quote

resisted such a change and cautioned that it would place control of Bitcoin in the hands of the companies that were pushing for the ostensible upgrade. They also warned that increasing the block size would diminish Bitcoin's decentralization by necessitating the use of more costly hardware, driving less affluent participants away from the network. Small-blockers viewed Bitcoin not as a piece of software but as a protocol and emphasized the cost to the ecosystem that would come from modifying its rules. Even more importantly, small-blockers recognized that if it became easy to change one consensus rule, then all rules, including Bitcoin's block subsidy rule, would be easier to modify. Because demand for Bitcoin as a store of value rests largely on the credibility of its fixed-supply monetary policy, changing Bitcoin's block size would indirectly undermine that credibility.

The fierce debate between Bitcoin's two factions came to a head on August 1, 2017 when the big-blocker faction modified the software running on their computers to accommodate larger blocks, thus making it incompatible with the rest of Bitcoin's network. Computers running the new software were rejected from the original Bitcoin network and formed a second network of their own in a process known as a fork. The second network was known as Bitcoin Cash and had its own separate tokens that could be traded on the market. The question of Bitcoin's future then shifted from a debate internal to the Bitcoin community to the marketplace where bitcoins, using the exchange symbol BTC, and

Bitcoin Cash tokens, using the symbol BCH, would trade against each other in an economic test of which vision would attract the greatest investor demand. In the following years, the market overwhelmingly voted in favor of the original network and a vision of Bitcoin as a nonsovereign store of value. The Bitcoin Cash network faded into irrelevance, and its small community was wracked by continued infighting and further schisms.

DENOUEMENT

The market's support for the Bitcoin network with its original consensus rules made clear that Bitcoin's value lies more in its existence as a largely immutable protocol than as an upgradeable piece of software. As a protocol with fixed consensus rules, Bitcoin's block size and the number of transactions that can be supported per block will remain limited. Growing adoption of Bitcoin will result in increasing demand for the limited space per block for transactions, implying that transaction fees must rise over time. Bitcoin's network will thus become uneconomical for small payments such as the purchase of coffee or bread but will remain suitable for settlement of the type of large value transfers that underpin a global financial system. Smaller payments with bitcoins will happen on layers built on top of the Bitcoin network such as the Lightning network or custodial transfer layers like banks. Hal Finney, the brilliant cryptographer who was first to recognize the potential of Satoshi Nakamoto's invention, wrote in 2010:

Bitcoin itself cannot scale to have every single financial transaction in the world be broadcast to everyone and included in the block chain. There needs to be a secondary level of payment systems which is lighter weight and more efficient.

...

I believe this will be the ultimate fate of Bitcoin, to be the "high-powered money" that serves as a reserve currency for banks that issue their own digital cash.[48]

Finney implicitly recognized that Bitcoin would first need to be established as a store of value, or reserve currency as he called it. Once established, bitcoins could be used for everyday payments using higher-layer systems. He understood that Bitcoin would not serve as a payment system competing directly with Visa or PayPal, but as something far more significant: a nonsovereign store of value that would function as the monetary base for a new global financial system. This was the fate written into Bitcoin's DNA—its consensus rules—from the very beginning.

---

48   http://bullishcaseforbitcoin.com/references/finney-second-layer-quote

ACKNOWLEDGMENTS

WHEN I BEGAN WRITING *THE BULLISH CASE FOR BITCOIN* AS A long-form article in early 2017, the price of Bitcoin hovered around $1,000 and I hoped the article might help to explain the economic importance of this revolutionary technology to a few friends and perhaps even some Wall Street investors. I did not anticipate that the article would eventually be read by hundreds of thousands of people around the world and be translated into twenty different languages by volunteers. This unexpected readership can be explained in part by a growing demand to understand Bitcoin and its significance, but it can also be attributed to the invaluable help I received in crafting a text that is accessible and interesting to the layperson. In this regard I wish to express my gratitude to those who contributed to the creation of the original article and to the completion of this book, which it significantly expands upon.

First, I would like to thank Michael Saylor for writing the foreword to this book and for his generous efforts in providing free educational content through his charity, Saylor Academy. Second, I would like to thank @BitcoinUltras, a pseudonymous artist that I met on Twitter, who volunteered to create the cover art and the beautiful art that adorns each chapter. Third, I would like to thank my friend Sanjay Mavinkurve who generously created the charts for this book, which epitomize the aphorism that a picture is worth a thousand words. I would like to thank Daniel Coleman, Michael Hartl, Ben Davenport, Mat Balez, and Stephan Kinsella for the diligence they showed in editing my manuscript. Numerous people provided feedback that improved the clarity of my writing, and for this I wish to thank Alex Morcos, John Pfeffer, Pierre Rochard, Koen Swinkels, Ray Boyapati, Michael Angelo, Patri Friedman, Ardian Tola, and Michael Flaxman.

Finally, and most importantly, I wish to thank my wife Lisa for helping me to see this project through and for providing me with the three greatest inspirations in my life, my darling children.

DISCLAIMER

The views presented in this book and any errors herein are my own. This book is for information purposes only. It is not intended to be investment advice. Seek a duly licensed professional for investment advice.

ABOUT THE AUTHOR

BORN AND RAISED IN AUSTRALIA, VIJAY BOYAPATI MOVED TO the United States in 2000 to pursue a PhD in Computer Science. Instead of enrolling in a doctoral program, Boyapati ended up at a small startup called Google where he spent several years using his background in machine learning to improve the ranking algorithms used in Google News. Boyapati left his lucrative job in 2007 to work on a grassroots campaign in the 2008 Presidential election, helping to raise millions of dollars and bring hundreds of volunteers to New Hampshire to canvass for Ron Paul. In 2011, Boyapati discovered Bitcoin and went down the proverbial rabbit hole in a quest to understand how a new form of Internet money, backed by no commodity and guaranteed by no government, could have any economic value. Armed with a background in Austrian economics, Boyapati penned "The Bullish Case for Bitcoin" as a long-form article in 2017 to provide the layperson with an economic framework with which they could understand Bitcoin.

Vijay Boyapati has a Bachelor of Science with first class honors from the Australian National University, receiving the University's highest undergraduate honor, the University Medal. He is a husband and loving father of Addie, Will, and Vivi. He lives with his family in Seattle, Washington.

INDEX

WWW.BULLISHCASEFORBITCOIN.COM

CPSIA information can be obtained
at www.ICGtesting.com
Printed in the USA
BVHW081213261021
619917BV00009B/304